SQL in MySQL

Learn and Practice

By

Suripeddi Koundinya

M.Tech. Biotechnology
M.A. Psychology
M.A. Astrology

2022 JUNE

<u>Contents</u>

<u>SQL vs MySQL: Key Difference</u>

SQL extends for Structured Query Language that enables the user to design and manage databases, while MySQL is a Relational database management system that allows a user to store and retrieve data from the database.

SQL is a standard language for retrieving and manipulating structured databases. On the contrary, MySQL is a relational database management system, like SQL Server, Oracle or IBM DB2, that is used to manage SQL databases.

Both the technologies work on the concept of storing data as per schema (table storage). MySQL is inclined more towards selecting the data to facilitate data display, update and save the data again. It is a bit weaker than SQL Server in terms of data insertion and deletion.

Many famous web-based applications and companies use MySQL like WordPress, YouTube, Joomla, etc. SQL is also used by many platforms like MYSQL, Oracle, Microsoft SQL Server, etc.

<u>Advantages of SQL</u>:

<u>Faster Query Processing</u>: Large amount of data is retrieved quickly and efficiently.

<u>No Coding Skills</u>: For data retrieval, large number of lines of code is not required.

<u>Standardized Language:</u> Due to documentation and long establishment over years, it provides a uniform platform worldwide to all its users.

<u>Portable:</u> It can be used in programs in PCs, server, laptops independent of any platform (Operating System, etc).

<u>Interactive Language:</u> Easy to learn and understand, answers to complex queries can be received in seconds.

<u>Multiple data views</u>

Advantages of MySQL:

<u>Flexibility:</u> MySQL runs on all operating systems

<u>Power:</u> MySQL focuses on performance

<u>Enterprise-Level SQL Features:</u> MySQL had for some time been lacking in advanced features such as subqueries, views, and stored procedures.

<u>Full-Text Indexing and Searching</u>

<u>Query Caching:</u> This helps enhance the speed of MySQL greatly

<u>Replication:</u> One MySQL server can be duplicated on another, providing numerous advantages

<u>Configuration and Security</u>.

SQL	MySQL
SQL is developed by Microsoft Corporation.	MySQL is combination of "My", the name of co-founder Michael Widenius's daughter, and "SQL", the abbreviation for Structured Query Language now owned and managed by Oracle Corporation.
SQL is a structured query language used for managing and retrieving data from the database system.	MySQL is a Relational database system that uses SQL to query data from the databases.
The syntax and format are fixed, declarative, and easy to use. Start with the clause and end with a semicolon.	MySQL is software and not a programming language, hence it does not have any commands or particular format.
SQL is proprietary based software owned by Microsoft and not open to others for free.	MySQL is an open-source free platform that allows access to any and everyone.
SQL was built for WIndows, works partially for Linux, macOS with its latest versions.	MySQL is adaptable for cross-platforms, working well for Linux, macOS, Windows.
SQL is in itself a programming language used for database systems.	MySQL supports all the basic programming languages like C, C++, Perl, PHP, Python, Ruby, and many others.

SQL supports only a single storage engine for different operations.	MySQL supports different storage engines and does not take up a lot of space for different functions and operations.
SQL servers are secured as no third party or outsiders are allowed to manipulate data.	MySQL is susceptible to more security threats due to its open-source nature. It gives access to data manipulation and modification to unauthorized users as well during the run-time.
In SQL, the server and database work independently. This allows users or interested parties to work on databases even during recovery sessions.	MySQL servers do not work independently from databases and hence, blocks the time for the users to do anything else.
Time consumed for data restoration in SQL is less for a large amount of data.	In MySQL, the process of data restoration is quite time-consuming and requires a number of SQL statements for the same.
SQL allows truncating a query even during execution without disabling the whole process.	MySQL does not allow you to cancel a query in the middle of execution.
SQL is available in different languages.	MySQL is available only in a single language that is English.
SQL does not come up or support any connectors.	MySQL supports connectors like WorkBench Tool for building databases.

SQL supports user-defined functions and XML.	MySQL does not support any user-defined function and XML.
The only support for SQL problems and queries is Microsoft Support care due to its highly protective usage.	MySQL has great community support as it allows free access.
Default ports for SQL Server are 1433 & 1434.	Default port for MySQL is 3306.
SQL Server worked faster than MySQL for DELETE, UPDATE, and SELECT queries.	For the INSERT operations, MySQL worked faster than SQL Server.
1103 companies reportedly use Microsoft SQL Server in their tech stacks, including Accenture, Hepsiburada, Stack Overflow, Alibaba Travels, Intuit, doubleSlash,etc	Some organizations using MySQL include Facebook, Netflix, Twitter, NASA, GitHub, YouTube, etc.
It is written in C and C++ languages.	It is also written in C and C++.
Supports row-based filtering which filters out the records on a database by database way. Gives the advantage of filtering multiple rows without considering a number of databases.	Allows to filter out the tables, rows, and users in a variety of ways. However, MySQL supports filtering only on individual database basis

In SQL Server, while backing up the data, the database is not blocked. This allows users to complete the backup and data restoration process completed in less time and efforts.	Backup of the data can be taken by extricating all the data as SQL statements. During the backup process, the database is blocked. This prevents the instances of data corruption while migrating from one version of MySQL to another.
Since this is a language, it does not get updates. SQL commands always remain the same.	Since it's a software, it gets frequent updates.

SQL is a 4th generation programming language which is multi-paradigm in nature. It is a declarative language and also contains procedural elements. It was initially released in the year 1986 and since then it became the most widely used database language. The latest version of SQL is SQL 2016. SQL follows the ISO/IEC 9075 standard.

MySQL is an open source RDBMS developed by MySQL AB (now Oracle Corporation) in 1995. Its latest stable release of version 8.0.15 happened in February 2019. It offers dual licensing distribution.

What is Database?

Data usually comes through raw format in an unorganized manner and processing of such data is called '**Information**'.

Our Data are stored in Databases [db] consists set of **Tables (Rows & Columns).** A Table is an organized collection of data stored in the form of Rows and Columns. Columns can be categorized as vertical, while Rows as horizontal. The Columns in a table are called Fields in records while the Rows can be referred to as unique Records.

For example, a Table that contains Employee data for a company might contain a row for each employee and columns representing employee information such as employee number, name, address, job title, etc.

A Computer can have one or more than one instance of SQL Server installed. Each instance of SQL Server can contain one or many databases. Within a database, there are one or many object ownership groups called schemas. Within each schema there are database objects such as tables, views, and stored procedures. Some objects such as certificates and asymmetric keys are contained within the database, but are not contained within a schema.

SQL Server databases are stored in the file system in files. Files can be grouped into file-groups.

At a minimum, every SQL Server database has two operating system files: a data file and a log file. Data files contain data and objects such as tables, indexes, stored procedures, and views. Log files contain the information that is required to recover all transcations in the database. Data files can be grouped together in file-groups for allocation and administration purposes.

The number of tables in a database is limited only by the number of objects allowed in a database (2,147,483,647). A standard user-defined table can have up to 1,024 columns. The number of rows in the table is limited only by the storage capacity of the server.

Rules to create Database:

a) Must accumulate Mass Storage.
b) Should Remove Duplicate Data.
c) Multiple Users can access Database.
d) Protect your data.

Users are required to do regular tasks of managing / manipulating data in a System or Server box which is called **Database Management System (DBMS).**

Different types of DBMS:

1) Centralized DBMS *(Multiple Users access the Data in central level)*
2) Distributed DBMS *(Multiple Databases distributed across different locations can access by Multiple Users)*
3) Cloud Database *(Databases hosted in the Cloud e.g. Maria DB, Azure SQL)*
4) Personal Database *(for Personal use)*
5) Relational Database *(e.g. RDBMS like MySQL)*
6) Commercial Database *(these are Premium or Pro version not Open Source -- e.g. Oracle, Mongo DB)*

7) Graph Database *(creating and manipulating graphs – (e.g. Neo4j, ArangoDB)*

Besides the standard role of basic user-defined tables, SQL Server provides the following types of tables that serve special purposes in a database:

a) Partitioned tables are tables whose data is horizontally divided into units which may be spread across more than one filegroup in a database. Partitioning makes large tables or indexes more manageable by letting you access or manage subsets of data quickly and efficiently, while maintaining the integrity of the overall collection. By default, SQL Server supports up to 15,000 partitions.

b) Temporary tables are stored in **tempdb**. There are two types of temporary tables: local and global. They differ from each other in their names, their visibility, and their availability.

Local temporary tables have a single number sign (#) as the first character of their names hey are visible only to the current connection for the user, and they are deleted when the user disconnects from the instance of SQL Server.

Global temporary tables have two number signs (##) as the first characters of their names; they are visible to any user after they are created, and they are deleted when all users referencing the table disconnect from the instance of SQL Server.

SQL in RDBMS

RDBMS (Relational Database Management System) is one of the types of DBMS which shows Relational between the Tables (where data are stored in the form of ROWS & COLUMNS).

In other words, Relational database is a type of database that allows us to identify and access data in relation to another piece of data in the database. It stores data in rows and columns in a series of tables to make processing and querying efficient.

Rows (Tuples) are Horizontal while Columns (Headers are called Attributes – ID, Name, etc.) are Vertical in a Table.

Degree of Relation = No. of Columns
Cardinality = No. of Rows
Data present inside the Column is called 'Domain Values'.

Objectives for creating the Tables:

    a) Every table must have a Unique Name.
    b) Every Cell must have a Single Value.
    c) Each Column must have a Distinct Name.
    d) No Duplicates in a Row.

Different types of RDBMS and their usage in some Companies:

    1) MySQL *(e.g.: Bank of England)*
    2) Oracle *(e.g.: Bank of America)*
    3) NETEZA
    4) SQL Server Management
    5) MS SQL *(e.g.: Cognizant)*
    6) Informix *(e.g.: Walmart)*
    7) Postgre SQL *(e.g.: MBRDI Mercedes Benz)*

Application of RDBMS:

a) Business
b) Airlines
c) Retail
d) Education

Language used to process (update / insert / delete) the data in RDBMS is called '**Structured / Standard Query Language (SQL)"**.

SQL uses in RDBMS:

a) Execute the queries.
b) Retrieve the data
c) Insert the data
d) Update the data
e) Delete the data
f) Create new database
g) Create new tables
h) Create new stored procedures
i) Create views in SQL

Different types of SQL statements:

A) **DDL (Data Definition Language)** are instructions like CREATE, DROP, ALTER & TRUNCATE.
B) **DML (Data Manipulation Language)** which are INSERT, UPDATE & DELETE.
C) **DQL (Data Query Language)** → SELECT.
D) **TCL (Transaction Control Language)** → COMMIT, ROLLBACK & SAVEPOINT.
E) **DCL (Data Control Language)** use by Admins which are GRANT & REVOKE.

How to create a Table in MySQL

1) First you need to create a Database:

```
mysql> create database suripeddi_Class10;
Query OK, 1 row affected (0.14 sec)
```

2) Go inside the database by using 'use' command:

```
mysql> use suripeddi_Class10;
Database changed
```

3) Check whether you have any tables inside database:

```
mysql> show tables;
Empty set (0.22 sec)
```

4) Now create a Table in RDBMS:

A table consists of a Unique Name which includes ID / Age followed by Integer, Name & Location followed by Varchar and Date as an example.

```
mysql> create table students(S_ID int,S_NAME varchar(200),S_AGE int,S_JOINDATE Date,S_LOC varchar(200));
Query OK, 0 rows affected (0.13 sec)
```

5) Check whether Table got created or not:

```
mysql> show tables;
+----------------------------+
| Tables_in_suripeddi_class10 |
+----------------------------+
| students                   |
+----------------------------+
1 row in set (0.01 sec)
```

6) <u>Now insert values and character (data) into the table:</u>

```
mysql> insert into students values(1,"Krishna",35,'2022-03-01',"Hyderabad");
Query OK, 1 row affected (0.05 sec)
```

```
mysql> select * from students;
+-------+---------+-------+-------------+-----------+
| S_ID  | S_NAME  | S_AGE | S_JOINDATE  | S_LOC     |
+-------+---------+-------+-------------+-----------+
|     1 | Krishna |    35 | 2022-03-01  | Hyderabad |
+-------+---------+-------+-------------+-----------+
1 row in set (0.00 sec)
```

So, we have converted Unstructured data into Structured data which is present along with Schema (given table below).

Schema is nothing but a structure of a table.

```
mysql> desc students;
+------------+--------------+------+-----+---------+-------+
| Field      | Type         | Null | Key | Default | Extra |
+------------+--------------+------+-----+---------+-------+
| S_ID       | int          | YES  |     | NULL    |       |
| S_NAME     | varchar(200) | YES  |     | NULL    |       |
| S_AGE      | int          | YES  |     | NULL    |       |
| S_JOINDATE | date         | YES  |     | NULL    |       |
| S_LOC      | varchar(200) | YES  |     | NULL    |       |
+------------+--------------+------+-----+---------+-------+
5 rows in set (0.04 sec)
```

7) <u>Now change the structure of the table by using command "alter":</u>

```
mysql> alter table students ADD(S_COUNTRY varchar(200));
Query OK, 0 rows affected (0.06 sec)
Records: 0  Duplicates: 0  Warnings: 0
```

```
mysql> desc students;
+------------+--------------+------+-----+---------+-------+
| Field      | Type         | Null | Key | Default | Extra |
+------------+--------------+------+-----+---------+-------+
| S_ID       | int          | YES  |     | NULL    |       |
| S_NAME     | varchar(200) | YES  |     | NULL    |       |
| S_AGE      | int          | YES  |     | NULL    |       |
| S_JOINDATE | date         | YES  |     | NULL    |       |
| S_LOC      | varchar(200) | YES  |     | NULL    |       |
| S_COUNTRY  | varchar(200) | YES  |     | NULL    |       |
+------------+--------------+------+-----+---------+-------+
6 rows in set (0.00 sec)
```

```
mysql> select * from students;
+------+--------+-------+------------+-----------+-----------+
| S_ID | S_NAME | S_AGE | S_JOINDATE | S_LOC     | S_COUNTRY |
+------+--------+-------+------------+-----------+-----------+
|    1 | Krishna|    35 | 2022-03-01 | Hyderabad | NULL      |
+------+--------+-------+------------+-----------+-----------+
1 row in set (0.00 sec)
```

8) <u>Use 'truncate' command to delete all the rows from the table</u>:

```
mysql> truncate table students;
Query OK, 0 rows affected (0.07 sec)

mysql> select * from students;
Empty set (0.01 sec)
```

Now you can see that table has been successfully removed except Schema.

9) <u>Use 'drop' command to delete entire table</u>:

```
mysql> drop table students;
Query OK, 0 rows affected (0.05 sec)

mysql> select * from students;
ERROR 1146 (42S02): Table 'suripeddi_class10.students' doesn't exist
```

Now table has been entirely deleted including schema and data.

10) <u>Type "system cls" to refresh</u>:

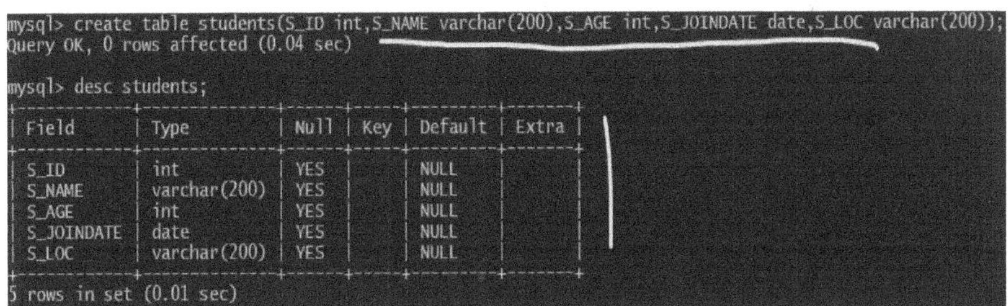

Now Create a Table Again

Use 'create table students(S_ID int,S_NAME varchar(200),S_AGE int,S_JOINDATE date,S_LOC varchar(200));'

Type 'insert into students(S_ID,S_NAME,S_AGE,S_JOINDATE,S_LOC) values(1,"Krishna",35,"2022-03-01","Hyderabad");'

Above syntax for inserting single column value.

To insert multiple values, use

insert into students values(2,"Shiva",36,'2022-04-01',"Chennai"),(3,"Brahma",37,'2022-05-01',"Mumbai");

To check whether data has been properly inserted or not, you need to give data query language – select * from students;

```
mysql> select * from students;
+-------+----------+--------+--------------+------------+
| S_ID  | S_NAME   | S_AGE  | S_JOINDATE   | S_LOC      |
+-------+----------+--------+--------------+------------+
|     1 | Krishna  |     35 | 2022-03-01   | Hyderabad  |
|     2 | Shiva    |     36 | 2022-04-01   | Chennai    |
|     3 | Brahma   |     37 | 2022-05-01   | Mumbai     |
+-------+----------+--------+--------------+------------+
3 rows in set (0.00 sec)
```

11) <u>Use 'update' command to change the value in particular column:</u>

```
mysql> update students set S_AGE=43 where S_ID=2;
Query OK, 1 row affected (0.01 sec)
Rows matched: 1  Changed: 1  Warnings: 0

mysql> select * from students;
+-------+----------+--------+--------------+------------+
| S_ID  | S_NAME   | S_AGE  | S_JOINDATE   | S_LOC      |
+-------+----------+--------+--------------+------------+
|     1 | Krishna  |     35 | 2022-03-01   | Hyderabad  |
|     2 | Shiva    |     43 | 2022-04-01   | Chennai    |
|     3 | Brahma   |     37 | 2022-05-01   | Mumbai     |
+-------+----------+--------+--------------+------------+
3 rows in set (0.00 sec)
```

12) <u>Use 'delete' command to remove particular Row:</u>

```
mysql> delete from students where S_ID=3;
Query OK, 1 row affected (0.01 sec)

mysql> select * from students;
+-------+----------+--------+--------------+------------+
| S_ID  | S_NAME   | S_AGE  | S_JOINDATE   | S_LOC      |
+-------+----------+--------+--------------+------------+
|     1 | Krishna  |     35 | 2022-03-01   | Hyderabad  |
|     2 | Shiva    |     43 | 2022-04-01   | Chennai    |
+-------+----------+--------+--------------+------------+
2 rows in set (0.00 sec)
```

13) Use following commands to get back the existing data (TCL):

a) '**begin work**' – take control by MySQL server of your data. This is very important command while performing DML operations.

b) '**rollback**' – to retrieve the deleted data. This command should use after 'begin work' only.

c) '**commit**' – to save the transaction to the database. You cannot do rollback once you commit the data.

Let's see with an example:

```
mysql>  begin work;
Query OK, 0 rows affected (0.00 sec)
```

```
mysql> delete from students where S_ID=2;
Query OK, 1 row affected (0.02 sec)
```

```
mysql> commit;
Query OK, 0 rows affected (0.01 sec)
```

```
mysql> select * from students;
+------+---------+-------+------------+-----------+
| S_ID | S_NAME  | S_AGE | S_JOINDATE | S_LOC     |
+------+---------+-------+------------+-----------+
|    1 | Krishna |    35 | 2022-03-01 | Hyderabad |
+------+---------+-------+------------+-----------+
1 row in set (0.00 sec)
```

Note: Lock in DB will happen if you forgot to mention 'commit' after 'begin work'.

Grant and Revoke access commands will be done by Admins only not users.

SQL is built on a database while Hive is built on file system, but both execute same on queries wise.

SQL Constraints

SQL constraints are conditions / rules that apply on the data columns of a table which is used to limit the type of data that goes inside the table.

Constraints are used to specify the rules concerning data in the table. It can be applied for single or multiple fields in an SQL table during the creation of the table or after creating using the ALTER TABLE command.

There are 3 types of Constraints:
- A) Key Constraint
- B) Domain Constraint
- C) Referential Integrity Constraint

The **PRIMARY KEY** constraint uniquely identifies each row in a table. It must contain UNIQUE values and has an implicit NOT NULL constraint.
A table in SQL is strictly restricted to have one and only one primary key, which is comprised of single or multiple fields (columns).

A **UNIQUE** constraint ensures that all values in a column are different. This provides uniqueness for the column(s) and helps identify each row uniquely. Unlike primary key, there can be multiple unique constraints defined per table. The code syntax for UNIQUE is quite similar to that of PRIMARY KEY and can be used interchangeably.

A **FOREIGN KEY** comprises of single or collection of fields in a table that essentially refers to the PRIMARY KEY in another table. Foreign key constraint ensures referential integrity in the relation between two tables.

The table with the foreign key constraint is labelled as the child table, and the table containing the candidate key is labelled as the referenced or parent table.

CONSTRAINTS	Uses
NOT NULL	Restricts NULL value from being inserted into a column.
CHECK	Verifies that all values in a field satisfy a condition.
DEFAULT	Automatically assigns a default value if no value has been specified for the field.
UNIQUE	Ensures unique values to be inserted into the field.
INDEX	Indexes a field providing faster retrieval of records.
PRIMARY KEY	Uniquely identifies each record (row) in a table.
FOREIGN KEY	Ensures referential integrity for a record in another table.

```
mysql> use world;
Database changed
mysql> select * from city limit 15;
+----+----------------+-------------+---------------+------------+
| ID | Name           | CountryCode | District      | Population |
+----+----------------+-------------+---------------+------------+
|  1 | Kabul          | AFG         | Kabol         |    1780000 |
|  2 | Qandahar       | AFG         | Qandahar      |     237500 |
|  3 | Herat          | AFG         | Herat         |     186800 |
|  4 | Mazar-e-Sharif | AFG         | Balkh         |     127800 |
|  5 | Amsterdam      | NLD         | Noord-Holland |     731200 |
|  6 | Rotterdam      | NLD         | Zuid-Holland  |     593321 |
|  7 | Haag           | NLD         | Zuid-Holland  |     440900 |
|  8 | Utrecht        | NLD         | Utrecht       |     234323 |
|  9 | Eindhoven      | NLD         | Noord-Brabant |     201843 |
| 10 | Tilburg        | NLD         | Noord-Brabant |     193238 |
| 11 | Groningen      | NLD         | Groningen     |     172701 |
| 12 | Breda          | NLD         | Noord-Brabant |     160398 |
| 13 | Apeldoorn      | NLD         | Gelderland    |     153491 |
| 14 | Nijmegen       | NLD         | Gelderland    |     152463 |
| 15 | Enschede       | NLD         | Overijssel    |     149544 |
+----+----------------+-------------+---------------+------------+
15 rows in set (0.09 sec)
```

As you can see above that No two Rows are similar to each other that means table should not contain duplicates. Otherwise, final output will change.

A) **<u>Key Constraint</u>**:

In order to stop duplicates enter into the table, we need to create a primary constraint which is called "Key Constraint". Example: Create table from an existing database.

```
mysql> show databases;
+--------------------+
| Database           |
+--------------------+
| information_schema |
| mysql              |
| performance_schema |
| sakila             |
| suripeddi_class10  |
| sys                |
| world              |
+--------------------+
7 rows in set (0.17 sec)

mysql> use suripeddi_class10;
Database changed
mysql> system cls;
```

```
Create table Persons (
ID INT,
LastName varchar (200),
FirstName varchar (200),
Age int,
PRIMARY KEY (ID)
);
```

```
mysql> Create table Persons (
    -> ID INT,
    -> LastName varchar (200),
    -> FirstName varchar (200),
    -> Age int,
    -> PRIMARY KEY (ID)
    -> );
Query OK, 0 rows affected (0.27 sec)

mysql> desc Persons;
+-----------+---------------+------+-----+---------+-------+
| Field     | Type          | Null | Key | Default | Extra |
+-----------+---------------+------+-----+---------+-------+
| ID        | int           | NO   | PRI | NULL    |       |
| LastName  | varchar(200)  | YES  |     | NULL    |       |
| FirstName | varchar(200)  | YES  |     | NULL    |       |
| Age       | int           | YES  |     | NULL    |       |
+-----------+---------------+------+-----+---------+-------+
4 rows in set (0.03 sec)

mysql>
```

PRIMARY KEY neither allows duplicates into the table nor NULL values into the Column.

Now insert data into the table.

```
        insert into Persons
values(1,"Suri","Meenu",18),(2,"Aya","Veda",24);
```

```
mysql> insert into Persons values(1,"Suri","Meenu",18),(2,"Aya","Veda",24);
Query OK, 2 rows affected (0.02 sec)
Records: 2  Duplicates: 0  Warnings: 0

mysql> select * from Persons;
+----+----------+-----------+------+
| ID | LastName | FirstName | Age  |
+----+----------+-----------+------+
|  1 | Suri     | Meenu     |   18 |
|  2 | Aya      | Veda      |   24 |
+----+----------+-----------+------+
2 rows in set (0.00 sec)
```

Now, try to insert a duplicate.

```
mysql> insert into Persons values(1,"Suri","Rama",18);
ERROR 1062 (23000): Duplicate entry '1' for key 'persons.PRIMARY'
```

See, Primary Key will not allow duplicates for Integers but not for varchar.

insert into persons values(3,"Dada","Victor",NULL);

```
mysql> select * from Persons;
+------+----------+-----------+------+
| ID   | LastName | FirstName | Age  |
+------+----------+-----------+------+
|    1 | Suri     | Meenu     |   18 |
|    2 | Aya      | Veda      |   24 |
|    3 | Dada     | Victor    | NULL |
+------+----------+-----------+------+
3 rows in set (0.00 sec)
```

Null Values are allowed in Age, etc., but not in Column ID (as you can see below)

```
mysql> insert into Persons values(NULL,"Dada","Victor",31);
ERROR 1048 (23000): Column 'ID' cannot be null
```

```
mysql> desc Persons;
+-----------+--------------+------+-----+---------+-------+
| Field     | Type         | Null | Key | Default | Extra |
+-----------+--------------+------+-----+---------+-------+
| ID        | int          | NO   | PRI | NULL    |       |
| LastName  | varchar(200) | YES  |     | NULL    |       |
| FirstName | varchar(200) | YES  |     | NULL    |       |
| Age       | int          | YES  |     | NULL    |       |
+-----------+--------------+------+-----+---------+-------+
4 rows in set (0.02 sec)
```

```
mysql> show tables;
+---------------------------+
| Tables_in_suripeddi_class10 |
+---------------------------+
| persons                   |
| students                  |
+---------------------------+
2 rows in set (0.01 sec)
```

See No PRI KEY in Students Table (see below)

```
mysql> desc students;
+-------------+--------------+------+-----+---------+-------+
| Field       | Type         | Null | Key | Default | Extra |
+-------------+--------------+------+-----+---------+-------+
| S_ID        | int          | YES  |     | NULL    |       |
| S_NAME      | varchar(200) | YES  |     | NULL    |       |
| S_AGE       | int          | YES  |     | NULL    |       |
| S_JOINDATE  | date         | YES  |     | NULL    |       |
| S_LOC       | varchar(200) | YES  |     | NULL    |       |
+-------------+--------------+------+-----+---------+-------+
5 rows in set (0.00 sec)
```

Use 'alter' & 'ADD PRIMARY KEY' commands for above Students table.

```
mysql> alter table students ADD PRIMARY KEY (S_ID);
Query OK, 0 rows affected (0.20 sec)
Records: 0  Duplicates: 0  Warnings: 0

mysql> desc students;
+-------------+--------------+------+-----+---------+-------+
| Field       | Type         | Null | Key | Default | Extra |
+-------------+--------------+------+-----+---------+-------+
| S_ID        | int          | NO   | PRI | NULL    |       |
| S_NAME      | varchar(200) | YES  |     | NULL    |       |
| S_AGE       | int          | YES  |     | NULL    |       |
| S_JOINDATE  | date         | YES  |     | NULL    |       |
| S_LOC       | varchar(200) | YES  |     | NULL    |       |
+-------------+--------------+------+-----+---------+-------+
5 rows in set (0.00 sec)
```

You can also remove PRI KEY by using "DROP" command

```
mysql> alter table students DROP PRIMARY KEY;
Query OK, 1 row affected (0.08 sec)
Records: 1  Duplicates: 0  Warnings: 0

mysql> desc students;
+-------------+--------------+------+-----+---------+-------+
| Field       | Type         | Null | Key | Default | Extra |
+-------------+--------------+------+-----+---------+-------+
| S_ID        | int          | NO   |     | NULL    |       |
| S_NAME      | varchar(200) | YES  |     | NULL    |       |
| S_AGE       | int          | YES  |     | NULL    |       |
| S_JOINDATE  | date         | YES  |     | NULL    |       |
| S_LOC       | varchar(200) | YES  |     | NULL    |       |
+-------------+--------------+------+-----+---------+-------+
5 rows in set (0.01 sec)
```

<u>Note</u>: A table will have only One Primary Key but can have more Unique Keys.

B) <u>**Referential Integrity Constraint (Foreign Key Constraint)**</u>

In order to relate two tables as ***parent-child relationship***, we need Foreign Key.

Let's say:

a) **Parent** → Persons *(ID is the Primary Key)*

b) *Child* → Orders *(OrderID is Primary Key while ID is the Foreign Key)*

First, create table Orders (

OrderID int,

OrderNumber int,

ID int,

PRIMARY KEY (OrderID),

FOREIGN KEY (ID) REFERENCES Persons(ID));

```
mysql> show databases;
+--------------------+
| Database           |
+--------------------+
| information_schema |
| mysql              |
| performance_schema |
| sakila             |
| suripeddi_class10  |
| sys                |
| world              |
+--------------------+
7 rows in set (0.00 sec)

mysql> use suripeddi_class10;
Database changed
mysql> show tables;
+-----------------------------+
| Tables_in_suripeddi_class10 |
+-----------------------------+
| persons                     |
| students                    |
+-----------------------------+
2 rows in set (0.00 sec)
```

Create table into Orders;

SQL in MySQL

```
mysql> create table Orders (
    -> OrderID int,
    -> OrderNumber int,
    -> ID int,
    -> PRIMARY KEY (OrderID),
    -> FOREIGN KEY (ID) REFERENCES Persons(ID));
Query OK, 0 rows affected (0.22 sec)
```

```
mysql> desc Orders;
+-------------+------+------+-----+---------+-------+
| Field       | Type | Null | Key | Default | Extra |
+-------------+------+------+-----+---------+-------+
| OrderID     | int  | NO   | PRI | NULL    |       |
| OrderNumber | int  | YES  |     | NULL    |       |
| ID          | int  | YES  | MUL | NULL    |       |
+-------------+------+------+-----+---------+-------+
3 rows in set (0.01 sec)
```

Select Persons tables;

```
mysql> select * from persons;
+----+----------+-----------+------+
| ID | LastName | FirstName | Age  |
+----+----------+-----------+------+
|  1 | Suri     | Meenu     |   18 |
|  2 | Aya      | Veda      |   24 |
|  3 | Dada     | Victor    | NULL |
+----+----------+-----------+------+
3 rows in set (0.00 sec)
```

```
mysql> insert into Orders values (1,2804,3),(2,4179,2),(3,8004,1);
Query OK, 3 rows affected (0.01 sec)
Records: 3  Duplicates: 0  Warnings: 0
```

```
mysql> select * from Orders;
+---------+-------------+------+
| OrderID | OrderNumber | ID   |
+---------+-------------+------+
|       1 |        2804 |    3 |
|       2 |        4179 |    2 |
|       3 |        8004 |    1 |
+---------+-------------+------+
3 rows in set (0.00 sec)
```

Now try to insert 4th table in Orders table;

```
mysql> insert into Orders values (4,6231,4);
ERROR 1452 (23000): Cannot add or update a child row: a foreign key constraint fails (`suripeddi_class10`.`orders`, CONSTRAINT `orders_ibfk_1` FOREIGN KEY (`ID`) REFERENCES `persons` (`ID`))
```

See as data ID is not present in Parent (Persons) tables, so not showing in Child (Orders) table.

Drop Foreign Key;

```
mysql> alter table Orders DROP FOREIGN KEY orders_ibfk_1;
Query OK, 0 rows affected (0.04 sec)
Records: 0  Duplicates: 0  Warnings: 0

mysql> desc Orders;
+-------------+------+------+-----+---------+-------+
| Field       | Type | Null | Key | Default | Extra |
+-------------+------+------+-----+---------+-------+
| OrderID     | int  | NO   | PRI | NULL    |       |
| OrderNumber | int  | YES  |     | NULL    |       |
| ID          | int  | YES  | MUL | NULL    |       |
+-------------+------+------+-----+---------+-------+
3 rows in set (0.01 sec)
```

Now you can see 4th Order ID (Child) after dropping Foreign Key.

```
mysql> insert into Orders values (4,6231,5);
Query OK, 1 row affected (0.00 sec)

mysql> select * from Orders;
+---------+-------------+------+
| OrderID | OrderNumber | ID   |
+---------+-------------+------+
|       1 |        2804 |    3 |
|       2 |        4179 |    2 |
|       3 |        8004 |    1 |
|       4 |        6231 |    5 |
+---------+-------------+------+
4 rows in set (0.00 sec)
```

C) <u>**Domain Constraint**</u>

Domain constraint defines a valid set of values for a table attribute also specifies all the possible values that the attribute can hold like integer, character, date, time, string, etc.

It is used to restrict the values to be inserted in the column or relation.

3   types of Domin Constriants:

a) NOT NULL constraint
b) Check constraint
c) UNIQUE constraint

a) __NOT NULL Constraint__:

If we specify a field in a table to be NOT NULL, then the field will never accept null value. That is, you will be not allowed to insert a new row in the table without specifying any value to this field.

```
create table Persons_NOTNULL (
ID int NOT NULL,
LastName varchar(200) NOT NULL,
FirstName varchar(200) NOT NULL,
Age int
);
```

```
mysql> create table Persons_NOTNULL (
    -> ID int NOT NULL,
    -> LastName varchar(200) NOT NULL,
    -> FirstName varchar(200) NOT NULL,
    -> Age int
    -> );
Query OK, 0 rows affected (0.06 sec)

mysql> desc Persons_NOTNULL;
+-----------+--------------+------+-----+---------+-------+
| Field     | Type         | Null | Key | Default | Extra |
+-----------+--------------+------+-----+---------+-------+
| ID        | int          | NO   |     | NULL    |       |
| LastName  | varchar(200) | NO   |     | NULL    |       |
| FirstName | varchar(200) | NO   |     | NULL    |       |
| Age       | int          | YES  |     | NULL    |       |
+-----------+--------------+------+-----+---------+-------+
4 rows in set (0.01 sec)
```

b) __UNIQUE Key Constraint__:

Provide uniqueness in table, ensures that all values in a column are different.

Create a table after choosing from available databases.

```
mysql> create table Persons_UK (
    -> ID int NOT NULL,
    -> LastName varchar(555) NOT NULL,
    -> FirstName varchar(555),
    -> Age int,
    -> CONSTRAINT UC_Persons UNIQUE(ID,LastName)
    -> );
Query OK, 0 rows affected (0.10 sec)
```

Describe Table to see the contents;

```
mysql> describe Persons_UK;
+-----------+--------------+------+-----+---------+-------+
| Field     | Type         | Null | Key | Default | Extra |
+-----------+--------------+------+-----+---------+-------+
| ID        | int          | NO   | PRI | NULL    |       |
| LastName  | varchar(555) | NO   | PRI | NULL    |       |
| FirstName | varchar(555) | YES  |     | NULL    |       |
| Age       | int          | YES  |     | NULL    |       |
+-----------+--------------+------+-----+---------+-------+
4 rows in set (0.01 sec)
```

See above table is showing 2 Primary Keys using Unique Key method.

Unique Key will not allow duplicates in both Cust_ID & Last_Name, means first 2 columns should be different.

c) **CHECK Constraint**: This ensures that all the values in a column satisfy certain conditions.

```
mysql> create table Persons_CK(
    -> ID int NOT NULL,
    -> LastName varchar(355) NOT NULL,
    -> FirstName varchar(355) NOT NULL,
    -> Age int,
    -> CHECK (Age > 25)
    -> );
Query OK, 0 rows affected (0.04 sec)
```

```
mysql> desc Persons_CK;
+-----------+--------------+------+-----+---------+-------+
| Field     | Type         | Null | Key | Default | Extra |
+-----------+--------------+------+-----+---------+-------+
| ID        | int          | NO   |     | NULL    |       |
| LastName  | varchar(355) | NO   |     | NULL    |       |
| FirstName | varchar(355) | NO   |     | NULL    |       |
| Age       | int          | YES  |     | NULL    |       |
+-----------+--------------+------+-----+---------+-------+
4 rows in set (0.00 sec)
```

Check constraint will not allow the age int less than 25.

```
mysql> insert into Persons_CK values (1,"Sai","krishna",50);
Query OK, 1 row affected (0.01 sec)

mysql> insert into Persons_CK values (2,"Gautam","krishna",24);
ERROR 3819 (HY000): Check constraint 'persons_ck_chk_1' is violated.
```

```
mysql> ALTER TABLE Persons_UK ADD CHECK ( Age >=18);
Query OK, 2 rows affected (0.07 sec)
Records: 2  Duplicates: 0  Warnings: 0
```

D) **<u>Auto Increment Constraint</u>**:

To automatically increase values in the table, mostly
Primary Key will be Auto Increment.

```
mysql> create table Persons_AI (
    -> ID int NOT NULL AUTO_INCREMENT,
    -> LastName varchar(255),
    -> FirstName varchar(255),
    -> Age int,
    -> PRIMARY KEY (ID)
    -> );
Query OK, 0 rows affected (0.04 sec)
```

```
mysql> desc Persons_AI;
+-----------+--------------+------+-----+---------+----------------+
| Field     | Type         | Null | Key | Default | Extra          |
+-----------+--------------+------+-----+---------+----------------+
| ID        | int          | NO   | PRI | NULL    | auto_increment |
| LastName  | varchar(255) | YES  |     | NULL    |                |
| FirstName | varchar(255) | YES  |     | NULL    |                |
| Age       | int          | YES  |     | NULL    |                |
+-----------+--------------+------+-----+---------+----------------+
4 rows in set (0.02 sec)
```

No need to give ID values.

```
mysql> insert into Persons_AI(LastName,FirstName,Age) values ("Surya","Kumar",36);
Query OK, 1 row affected (0.01 sec)

mysql> select * from Persons_AI;
+----+----------+-----------+------+
| ID | LastName | FIrstName | Age  |
+----+----------+-----------+------+
|  1 | Mahesh   | Sai       |   34 |
|  2 | Surya    | Kumar     |   36 |
+----+----------+-----------+------+
```

Operators in SQL

SQL Operators are special Words or Characters used to perform specific tasks both mathematical and logical computations on operands, which use 'WHERE' clause in a SQL query / statement.

There are six types of SQL operators that we are going to cover: Arithmetic, Bitwise, Comparison, Compound, Logical and String.

Every database administrator and user uses SQL queries for manipulating and accessing the data of database tables and views with the help of reserved words and characters, which are used to perform arithmetic operations, logical operations, comparison operations, compound operations, etc.

SQL Operators	Description
Arithmetic	Add (+), Subtract (-), Multiply (*), Divide (/), Modulo (%)
Bitwise	AND (&), OR (|), exclusive OR (^)
Comparison	Equal to (=), Greater than (>), Less than (<), Greater than or equal to (>=), Less than or equal to (<=), Not equal to (<>)
Compound	Add equals (+=), Subtract equals (-=), Multiply equals (*=), Divide equals (/=), Modulo equals (%=), Bitwise AND equals (&=), Bitwise exclusive equals (^-=), Bitwise OR equals (|*=)

Few Examples:

a) **'Not Equal' (<>) Operator:** The! = symbol is used to filter results that do not equal a certain value.

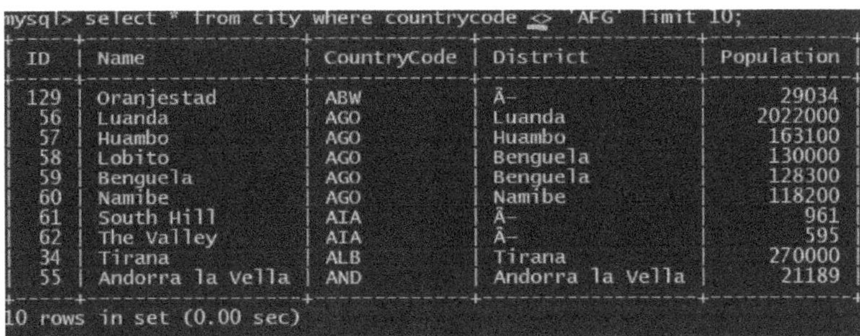

b) **'LIKE" Operator**: The LIKE operator searches for a specified pattern in a column.

This operator is used in the WHERE clause with the following three statements:

1. SELECT statement
2. UPDATE statement
3. DELETE statement

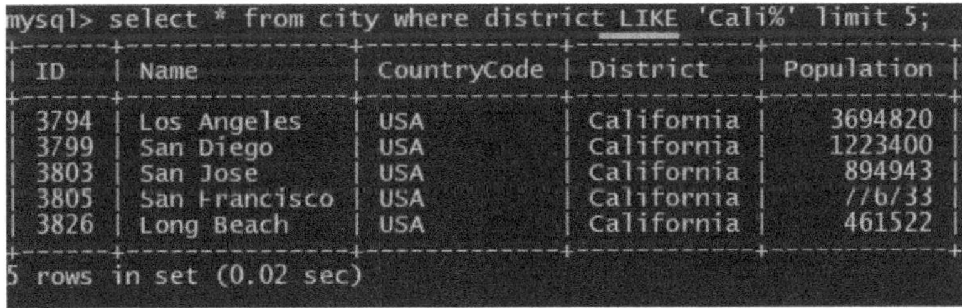

c) '**NOT LIKE**" **Operator**:

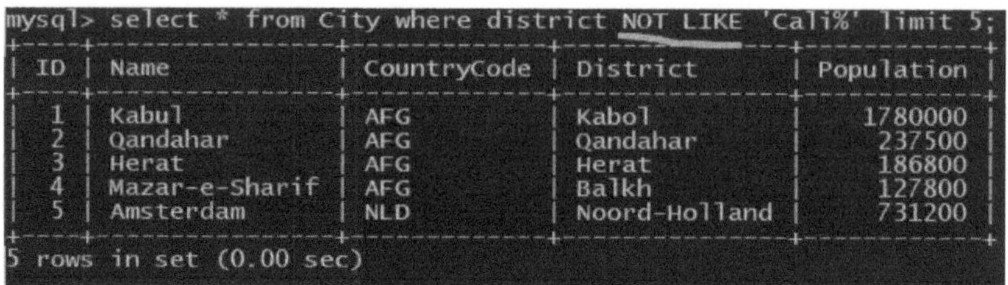

```
mysql> select * from City where district NOT LIKE 'Cali%' limit 5;
+------+----------------+-------------+---------------+------------+
| ID   | Name           | CountryCode | District      | Population |
+------+----------------+-------------+---------------+------------+
|    1 | Kabul          | AFG         | Kabol         |    1780000 |
|    2 | Qandahar       | AFG         | Qandahar      |     237500 |
|    3 | Herat          | AFG         | Herat         |     186800 |
|    4 | Mazar-e-Sharif | AFG         | Balkh         |     127800 |
|    5 | Amsterdam      | NLD         | Noord-Holland |     731200 |
+------+----------------+-------------+---------------+------------+
5 rows in set (0.00 sec)
```

d) '**IN' Operator**: in SQL allows database users to specify two or more values in a WHERE clause. This logical operator minimizes the requirement of multiple OR conditions.

```
mysql> select count(*) from city where countrycode in ('IND','USA');
+----------+
| count(*) |
+----------+
|      616 |
+----------+
1 row in set (0.00 sec)
```

Aggregate Functions in SQL

SQL aggregation function is used to perform the calculations on multiple rows of a single column of a table which returns a single value. It is also used to summarize the data. We often use aggregate functions with the GROUP BY, WHERE and HAVING clauses of the SELECT statement.

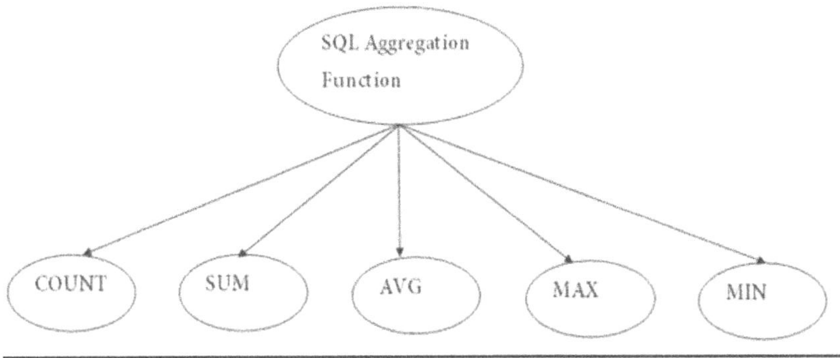

1) SUM:

Sum function is used to calculate the sum of all selected columns. It works on numeric fields only.

```
mysql> select sum(population) from city where countrycode='IND';
+-----------------+
| sum(population) |
+-----------------+
|       123298526 |
+-----------------+
1 row in set (0.00 sec)
```

2) COUNT:

COUNT function is used to Count the number of rows in a database table. It can work on both numeric and non-numeric data types.

```
mysql> select count(*) from city where countrycode = 'IND';
+----------+
| count(*) |
+----------+
|      341 |
+----------+
1 row in set (0.00 sec)
```

3) MAX:

MAX function is used to find the maximum value of a certain column. This function determines the largest value of all selected values of a column.

```
mysql> select max(population) from city where countrycode = 'IND';
+-----------------+
| max(population) |
+-----------------+
|        10500000 |
+-----------------+
1 row in set (0.01 sec)
```

4) MIN:

MIN function is used to find the minimum value of a certain column. This function determines the smallest value of all selected values of a column.

```
mysql> select min(population) from city where countrycode = 'IND';
+-----------------+
| min(population) |
+-----------------+
|           89053 |
+-----------------+
1 row in set (0.00 sec)
```

5) AVG:

The AVG function is used to calculate the average value of the numeric type. AVG function returns the average of all non-Null values.

```
mysql> select avg(population) from city where countrycode = 'IND';
+-----------------+
| avg(population) |
+-----------------+
|     361579.2551 |
+-----------------+
1 row in set (0.00 sec)
```

Temp Tables

As its name indicates, temporary tables are used to store data temporarily and they can perform CRUD (Create, Read, Update, and Delete).

Temp table will not exist once application has been closed.

```
mysql> desc student_temp;
+--------+--------------+------+-----+---------+-------+
| Field  | Type         | Null | Key | Default | Extra |
+--------+--------------+------+-----+---------+-------+
| S_ID   | int          | YES  |     | NULL    | NULL  |
| S_NAME | varchar(255) | YES  |     | NULL    | NULL  |
| S_Age  | int          | YES  |     | NULL    | NULL  |
+--------+--------------+------+-----+---------+-------+
3 rows in set (0.00 sec)

mysql> insert into student_temp values (1,"Sai",30);
Query OK, 1 row affected (0.00 sec)

mysql> insert into student_temp values (2,"Mahesh",22);
Query OK, 1 row affected (0.00 sec)
```

```
mysql> select * from student_temp;
+------+--------+-------+
| S_ID | S_NAME | S_Age |
+------+--------+-------+
|    1 | Sai    |    30 |
|    2 | Mahesh |    22 |
+------+--------+-------+
2 rows in set (0.00 sec)
```

Now, create a temporary table which has structure similar to production table.

```
mysql> select * from persons;
+----+----------+-----------+------+
| ID | LastName | FirstName | Age  |
+----+----------+-----------+------+
|  1 | Sai      | Mahesh    |   25 |
|  2 | Girish   | Kumar     |   24 |
|  3 | Ramesh   | Reddy     | NULL |
+----+----------+-----------+------+
3 rows in set (0.01 sec)

mysql> create temporary table persons_temp select * from persons;
Query OK, 3 rows affected (0.00 sec)
Records: 3  Duplicates: 0  Warnings: 0

mysql> select * from persons_temp;
+----+----------+-----------+------+
| ID | LastName | FirstName | Age  |
+----+----------+-----------+------+
|  1 | Sai      | Mahesh    |   25 |
|  2 | Girish   | Kumar     |   24 |
|  3 | Ramesh   | Reddy     | NULL |
+----+----------+-----------+------+
3 rows in set (0.00 sec)
```

In Back Up, only Schema is copied.

```
mysql> create temporary table persons_backup like persons;
Query OK, 0 rows affected (0.00 sec)

mysql> select * from persons_backup;
Empty set (0.00 sec)

mysql> desc persons_backup ;
+-----------+--------------+------+-----+---------+-------+
| Field     | Type         | Null | Key | Default | Extra |
+-----------+--------------+------+-----+---------+-------+
| ID        | int          | NO   | PRI | NULL    | NULL  |
| LastName  | varchar(200) | YES  |     | NULL    | NULL  |
| FirstName | varchar(200) | YES  |     | NULL    | NULL  |
| Age       | int          | YES  |     | NULL    | NULL  |
+-----------+--------------+------+-----+---------+-------+
4 rows in set (0.00 sec)
```

You can also Drop Temp table from table.

```
mysql> drop temporary table persons_backup;
Query OK, 0 rows affected (0.00 sec)

mysql> drop table persons_temp;
Query OK, 0 rows affected (0.00 sec)
```

Insert Data into another table using Select statement.

```
mysql> select * from persons;
+----+----------+-----------+------+
| ID | LastName | FirstName | Age  |
+----+----------+-----------+------+
|  1 | Sai      | Mahesh    |   25 |
|  2 | Girish   | Kumar     |   24 |
|  3 | Ramesh   | Reddy     | NULL |
+----+----------+-----------+------+
3 rows in set (0.00 sec)

mysql> create table Persons_info like persons;
Query OK, 0 rows affected (0.03 sec)

mysql> select * from persons;
+----+----------+-----------+------+
| ID | LastName | FirstName | Age  |
+----+----------+-----------+------+
|  1 | Sai      | Mahesh    |   25 |
|  2 | Girish   | Kumar     |   24 |
|  3 | Ramesh   | Reddy     | NULL |
+----+----------+-----------+------+
3 rows in set (0.00 sec)
```

```
mysql> insert into persons_info select * from persons where Age > 20;
Query OK, 2 rows affected (0.01 sec)
Records: 2  Duplicates: 0  Warnings: 0

mysql> select * from persons_info;
+----+----------+-----------+------+
| ID | LastName | FirstName | Age  |
+----+----------+-----------+------+
|  1 | Sai      | Mahesh    |   25 |
|  2 | Girish   | Kumar     |   24 |
```

Group By

Grouping the similar data is called 'Group By'.

The SQL **GROUP BY** clause is used in collaboration with the SELECT statement to arrange identical data into groups. This GROUP BY clause follows the WHERE clause in a SELECT statement and precedes the ORDER BY clause.

The GROUP BY statement is often used with aggregate functions (COUNT(), MAX(), MIN(), SUM(), AVG()) to group the result-set by one or more columns.

Display the count of each and every country.

```
mysql> select count(*),countrycode from city group by countrycode;
+----------+-------------+
| count(*) | countrycode |
+----------+-------------+
|        1 | ABW         |
|        4 | AFG         |
|        5 | AGO         |
|        2 | AIA         |
|        1 | ALB         |
|        1 | AND         |
|        1 | ANT         |
|        5 | ARE         |
|       57 | ARG         |
|        3 | ARM         |
|        2 | ASM         |
|        1 | ATG         |
```

```
mysql> select count(*) as cnt,countrycode from city group by countrycode order by cnt limit 10;
+-----+-------------+
| cnt | countrycode |
+-----+-------------+
|   1 | ABW         |
|   1 | BHR         |
|   1 | BDI         |
|   1 | BRN         |
|   1 | ALB         |
|   1 | AND         |
|   1 | ANT         |
|   1 | BRB         |
|   1 | ATG         |
|   1 | BHS         |
+-----+-------------+
10 rows in set (0.01 sec)
```

```
mysql> select count(*) as cnt,countrycode from city group by countrycode order by cnt desc limit 10;
+-----+-------------+
| cnt | countrycode |
+-----+-------------+
| 363 | CHN         |
| 341 | IND         |
| 274 | USA         |
| 250 | BRA         |
| 248 | JPN         |
| 189 | RUS         |
| 173 | MEX         |
| 136 | PHL         |
|  93 | DEU         |
|  85 | IDN         |
+-----+-------------+
10 rows in set (0.00 sec)
```

```
mysql> select sum(population) as 'sm_pop',countrycode from city group by countrycode order by sm_pop desc limit 10;
+-----------+-------------+
| sm_pop    | countrycode |
+-----------+-------------+
| 175953614 | CHN         |
| 123298526 | IND         |
|  85876862 | BRA         |
|  78625774 | USA         |
|  77965107 | JPN         |
|  69150700 | RUS         |
|  59752521 | MEX         |
|  38999893 | KOR         |
|  37485695 | IDN         |
|  31546745 | PAK         |
+-----------+-------------+
10 rows in set (0.02 sec)
```

Having Clause along with Group By

```
mysql> select sum(population) as 'sm_pop',countrycode from city group by countrycode having sm_pop > 1000000 order by sm_pop desc limit 10;
+-----------+-------------+
| sm_pop    | countrycode |
+-----------+-------------+
| 175953614 | CHN         |
| 123298526 | IND         |
|  85876862 | BRA         |
|  78625774 | USA         |
|  77965107 | JPN         |
|  69150700 | RUS         |
|  59752521 | MEX         |
|  38999893 | KOR         |
|  37485695 | IDN         |
|  31546745 | PAK         |
+-----------+-------------+
10 rows in set (0.02 sec)
```

```
mysql> select countrycode , count(*) as cnt from city group by countrycode having cnt > 300;
+-------------+-----+
| countrycode | cnt |
+-------------+-----+
| CHN         | 363 |
| IND         | 341 |
+-------------+-----+
2 rows in set (0.01 sec)
```

```
mysql> select * from city group by ID having count(ID) > 1;
Empty set (0.01 sec)

mysql>
```

"WHERE", "AND", "OR" Clauses in SQL

A **WHERE clause** in SQL is a data manipulation language statement. WHERE clause is used in SELECT, UPDATE, DELETE statement etc.

WHERE clauses are not mandatory clauses of SQL DML statements. But it can be used to limit the number of rows affected by a SQL DML statement or returned by a query.

The SQL **AND** condition is used in SQL query to create two or more conditions to be met. It is used in SQL **SELECT, INSERT, UPDATE** and **DELETE.**

The SQL **OR** condition is used in SQL query to create a SQL statement where records are returned when any one condition met. It can be used in a **SELECT** statement, **INSERT** statement, **UPDATE** statement or **DELETE** statement.

```
mysql> use world;
Database changed
mysql> select * from city limit 10;
+----+----------------+-------------+---------------+------------+
| ID | Name           | CountryCode | District      | Population |
+----+----------------+-------------+---------------+------------+
|  1 | Kabul          | AFG         | Kabol         |    1780000 |
|  2 | Qandahar       | AFG         | Qandahar      |     237500 |
|  3 | Herat          | AFG         | Herat         |     186800 |
|  4 | Mazar-e-Sharif | AFG         | Balkh         |     127800 |
|  5 | Amsterdam      | NLD         | Noord-Holland |     731200 |
|  6 | Rotterdam      | NLD         | Zuid-Holland  |     593321 |
|  7 | Haag           | NLD         | Zuid-Holland  |     440900 |
|  8 | Utrecht        | NLD         | Utrecht       |     234323 |
|  9 | Eindhoven      | NLD         | Noord-Brabant |     201843 |
| 10 | Tilburg        | NLD         | Noord-Brabant |     193238 |
+----+----------------+-------------+---------------+------------+
10 rows in set (0.16 sec)

mysql> select * from city where countrycode = 'IND';
```

ID	Name	CountryCode	District	Population
1024	Mumbai (Bombay)	IND	Maharashtra	10500000
1025	Delhi	IND	Delhi	7206704
1026	Calcutta [Kolkata]	IND	West Bengali	4399819
1027	Chennai (Madras)	IND	Tamil Nadu	3841396
1028	Hyderabad	IND	Andhra Pradesh	2964638
1029	Ahmedabad	IND	Gujarat	2876710
1030	Bangalore	IND	Karnataka	2660088
1031	Kanpur	IND	Uttar Pradesh	1874409
1032	Nagpur	IND	Maharashtra	1624752
1033	Lucknow	IND	Uttar Pradesh	1619115
1034	Pune	IND	Maharashtra	1566651
1035	Surat	IND	Gujarat	1498817
1036	Jaipur	IND	Rajasthan	1458483
1037	Indore	IND	Madhya Pradesh	1091674
1038	Bhopal	IND	Madhya Pradesh	1062771
1039	Ludhiana	IND	Punjab	1042740
1040	Vadodara (Baroda)	IND	Gujarat	1031346
1041	Kalyan	IND	Maharashtra	1014557
1042	Madurai	IND	Tamil Nadu	977856
1043	Haora (Howrah)	IND	West Bengali	950435
1044	Varanasi (Benares)	IND	Uttar Pradesh	929270

Use 'Where' & 'And' Clauses both

```
mysql> select * from city where CountryCode = 'IND' and population > 1000000;
```

ID	Name	CountryCode	District	Population
1024	Mumbai (Bombay)	IND	Maharashtra	10500000
1025	Delhi	IND	Delhi	7206704
1026	Calcutta [Kolkata]	IND	West Bengali	4399819
1027	Chennai (Madras)	IND	Tamil Nadu	3841396
1028	Hyderabad	IND	Andhra Pradesh	2964638
1029	Ahmedabad	IND	Gujarat	2876710
1030	Bangalore	IND	Karnataka	2660088
1031	Kanpur	IND	Uttar Pradesh	1874409
1032	Nagpur	IND	Maharashtra	1624752
1033	Lucknow	IND	Uttar Pradesh	1619115
1034	Pune	IND	Maharashtra	1566651
1035	Surat	IND	Gujarat	1498817
1036	Jaipur	IND	Rajasthan	1458483
1037	Indore	IND	Madhya Pradesh	1091674
1038	Bhopal	IND	Madhya Pradesh	1062771
1039	Ludhiana	IND	Punjab	1042740
1040	Vadodara (Baroda)	IND	Gujarat	1031346
1041	Kalyan	IND	Maharashtra	1014557

```
18 rows in set (0.00 sec)
```

```
mysql> select * from city where countrycode = 'IND' or population > 200000 limit 10;
+------+-----------+-------------+---------------+------------+
| ID   | Name      | CountryCode | District      | Population |
+------+-----------+-------------+---------------+------------+
|    1 | Kabul     | AFG         | Kabol         |    1780000 |
|    2 | Qandahar  | AFG         | Qandahar      |     237500 |
|    5 | Amsterdam | NLD         | Noord-Holland |     731200 |
|    6 | Rotterdam | NLD         | Zuid-Holland  |     593321 |
|    7 | Haag      | NLD         | Zuid-Holland  |     440900 |
|    8 | Utrecht   | NLD         | Utrecht       |     234323 |
|    9 | Eindhoven | NLD         | Noord-Brabant |     201843 |
|   34 | Tirana    | ALB         | Tirana        |     270000 |
|   35 | Alger     | DZA         | Alger         |    2168000 |
|   36 | Oran      | DZA         | Oran          |     609823 |
+------+-----------+-------------+---------------+------------+
10 rows in set (0.00 sec)
```

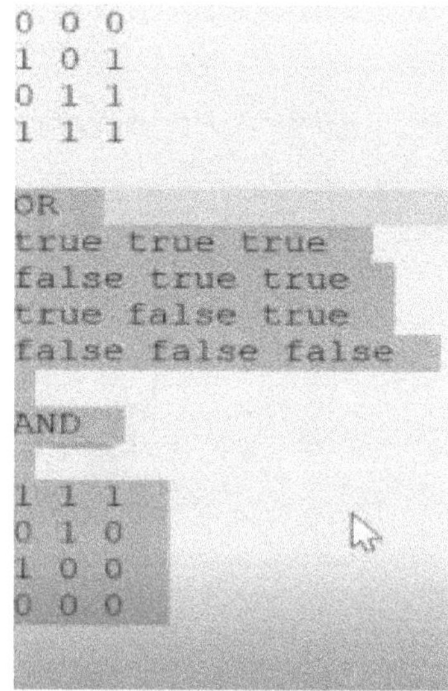

SQL JOINS

SQL Join statement is used to combine data or rows from two or more tables based on a common field between them. We use SQL Joins to access data from multiple tables.

There are 6 types of Joins:

1) INNER JOIN
2) OUTER JOIN
3) LEFT OUTER JOIN
4) RIGHT OUTER JOIN
5) CROSS JOIN
6) SELF JOIN

Here are the different types of the JOINs in SQL:

- (INNER) JOIN: Returns records that have matching values in both tables.
- LEFT (OUTER) JOIN: Returns all records from the left table, and the matched records from the right table.
- RIGHT (OUTER) JOIN: Returns all records from the right table, and the matched records from the left table.
- FULL (OUTER) JOIN: Returns all records when there is a match in either left or right table.

1) **INNER JOIN**:

We can Join 2 tables through the same Column Key. Here, we can match Data by joining 2 tables.

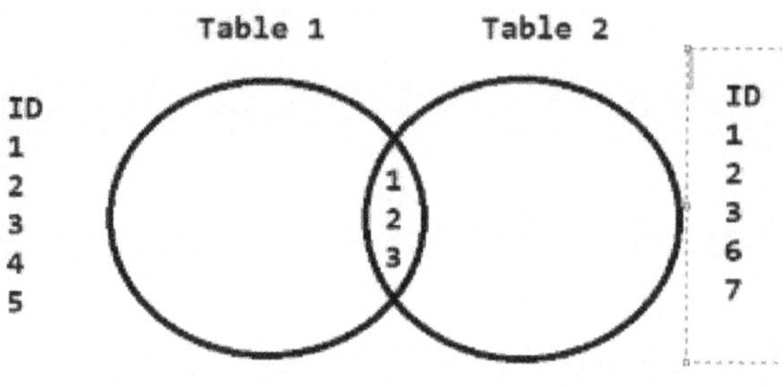

2) **LEFT OUTER JOIN**:

Here, not only you will get the data in the matching table after joining 2 tables, but also the data present only in the Left table.

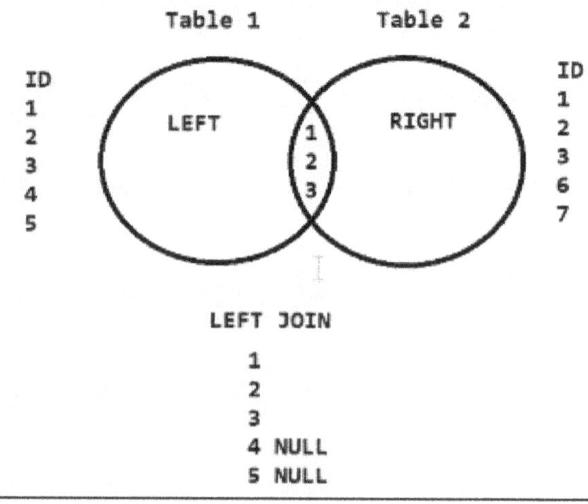

3) **<u>RIGHT OUTER JOIN:</u>**

Here we get matching data present in both the tables, but also the data present in Left Outer Join.

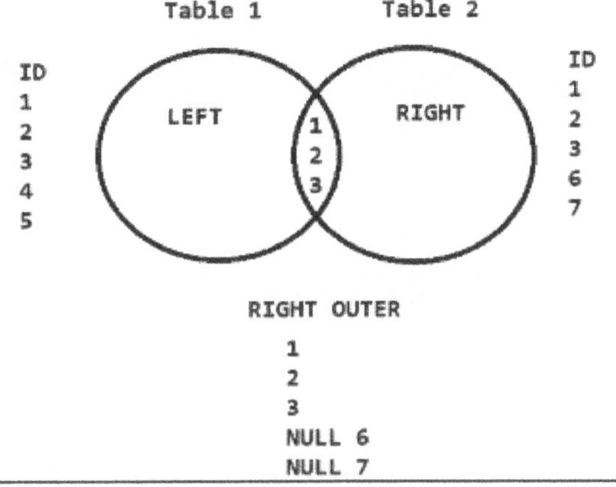

4) **<u>FULL OUTER JOIN</u>**:

Combination of Left and Right Outer Joins s called Full Outer Join.

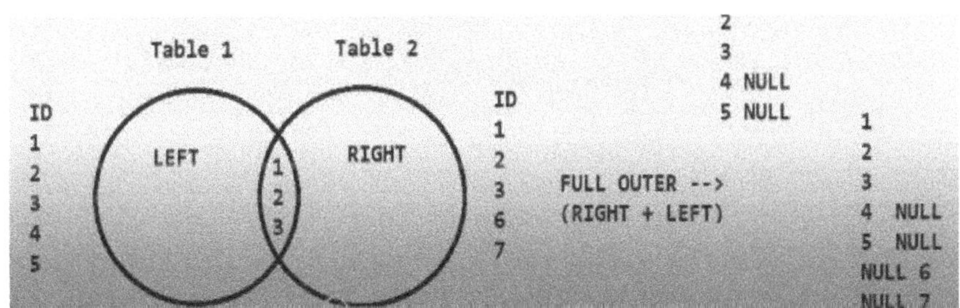

Here Example:

First Create Database in MySQL:

```
mysql> create database Suripeddi_c10_Joins;
Query OK, 1 row affected (0.06 sec)
```

<u>Use this Database:</u>

```
mysql> use Suripeddi_c10_Joins;
Database changed
```

<u>Create Table no. 1 inside Database:</u>

Create table Customer_Join(

    Customer_ID int NOT NULL,

    Customer_Name varchar(255) NOT NULL,

    Contact_Name varchar(255),

    Address varchar(255),

    postalcode INT,

    COUNTRY varchar(255),

    PRIMARY KEY (Customer_ID)

    );

```
mysql> Create table Customer_Join(
    -> Customer_ID int NOT NULL,
    -> Customer_Name varchar(255) NOT NULL,
    -> Contact_Name varchar(255),
    -> Address varchar(255),
    -> postalcode INT,
    -> COUNTRY varchar(255),
    -> PRIMARY KEY (Customer_ID)
    -> );
Query OK, 0 rows affected (0.25 sec)
```

<u>Describe table no.1 (Customer_Join):</u>

    Here Primary Key is Customer_ID.

```
mysql> describe Customer_Join;
+---------------+--------------+------+-----+---------+-------+
| Field         | Type         | Null | Key | Default | Extra |
+---------------+--------------+------+-----+---------+-------+
| Customer_ID   | int          | NO   | PRI | NULL    |       |
| Customer_Name | varchar(255) | NO   |     | NULL    |       |
| Contact_Name  | varchar(255) | YES  |     | NULL    |       |
| Address       | varchar(255) | YES  |     | NULL    |       |
| postalcode    | int          | YES  |     | NULL    |       |
| COUNTRY       | varchar(255) | YES  |     | NULL    |       |
+---------------+--------------+------+-----+---------+-------+
6 rows in set (0.08 sec)
```

Add Column into the Table:

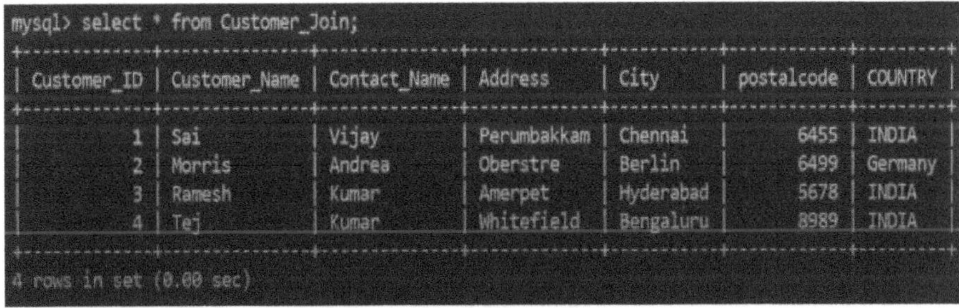

```
mysql> alter table Customer_Join add column(City varchar(255))
    -> ;
Query OK, 0 rows affected (0.04 sec)
Records: 0  Duplicates: 0  Warnings: 0

mysql> describe Customer_Join
    -> ;
+---------------+--------------+------+-----+---------+-------+
| Field         | Type         | Null | Key | Default | Extra |
+---------------+--------------+------+-----+---------+-------+
| Customer_ID   | int          | NO   | PRI | NULL    |       |
| Customer_Name | varchar(255) | NO   |     | NULL    |       |
| Contact_Name  | varchar(255) | YES  |     | NULL    |       |
| Address       | varchar(255) | YES  |     | NULL    |       |
| postalcode    | int          | YES  |     | NULL    |       |
| COUNTRY       | varchar(255) | YES  |     | NULL    |       |
| City          | varchar(255) | YES  |     | NULL    |       |
+---------------+--------------+------+-----+---------+-------+
7 rows in set (0.01 sec)
```

Insert Data into Tables:

insert into
Customer_Join(Customer_ID,Customer_Name,Contact_name,Addre
ss,postalcode,COUNTRY,city) values
(1,"Krishna","Suri","Mehdipatnam",5042,"India",Hyderabad");

Select * from Table;

```
mysql> select * from Customer_Join;
+-------------+---------------+--------------+-------------+-----------+------------+---------+
| Customer_ID | Customer_Name | Contact_Name | Address     | City      | postalcode | COUNTRY |
+-------------+---------------+--------------+-------------+-----------+------------+---------+
|           1 | Sai           | Vijay        | Perumbakkam | Chennai   |       6455 | INDIA   |
|           2 | Morris        | Andrea       | Oberstre    | Berlin    |       6499 | Germany |
|           3 | Ramesh        | Kumar        | Amerpet     | Hyderabad |       5678 | INDIA   |
|           4 | Tej           | Kumar        | Whitefield  | Bengaluru |       8989 | INDIA   |
+-------------+---------------+--------------+-------------+-----------+------------+---------+
4 rows in set (0.00 sec)
```

Create another Table Order_Join (table no.2):

```
mysql> create table Order_Join(
    -> Order_ID int not null,
    -> Customer_ID int NOT NULL,
    -> Employee_ID int NOT NULL,
    -> Order_Date date,
    -> shipper_ID int,
    -> PRIMARY KEY (Order_ID),
    -> CONSTRAINT FK_CustomerOrder FOREIGN KEY (Customer_ID) REFERENCES Customer_Join(Customer_ID));
Query OK, 0 rows affected (0.07 sec)
```

<u>Describe table no. 2 (Order_Join);</u>

```
mysql> describe order_Join;
+-------------+------+------+-----+---------+-------+
| Field       | Type | Null | Key | Default | Extra |
+-------------+------+------+-----+---------+-------+
| Order_ID    | int  | NO   | PRI | NULL    |       |
| Customer_ID | int  | NO   | MUL | NULL    |       |
| Employee_ID | int  | NO   |     | NULL    |       |
| Order_Date  | date | YES  |     | NULL    |       |
| shipper_ID  | int  | YES  |     | NULL    |       |
+-------------+------+------+-----+---------+-------+
5 rows in set (0.01 sec)
```

Here the

Primary Key in table no. 2 (Order_Join) is Order_ID.

Foreign Key is table no. 2 (Order_Join) is Customer_ID which is

Primary Key in table no.1.

We use Customer_ID as common Column to Join 2 Tables (1 & 2).

<u>Insert Data into table no.2 (Order_Join):</u>

<u>Select * from table no.2 (Order_Join):</u>

```
mysql> insert into Order_Join values(10309,3,3,'2020-01-02',1);
Query OK, 1 row affected (0.01 sec)

mysql> insert into Order_Join values(10310,1,3,'2020-01-02',1);
Query OK, 1 row affected (0.00 sec)

mysql> select * from order_join;
+----------+-------------+-------------+------------+------------+
| Order_ID | Customer_ID | Employee_ID | Order_Date | shipper_ID |
+----------+-------------+-------------+------------+------------+
|    10308 |           2 |           7 | 2020-01-01 |          3 |
|    10309 |           3 |           3 | 2020-01-02 |          1 |
|    10310 |           1 |           3 | 2020-01-02 |          1 |
+----------+-------------+-------------+------------+------------+
3 rows in set (0.00 sec)
```

<u>Select * from table no.1 (Customer_Join):</u>

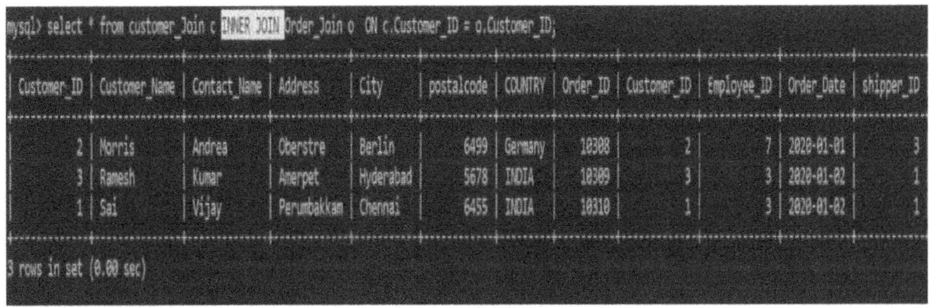

Join 2 tables to get Matching Data:

Select * from Customer_Join c INNER JOIN Order_Join o ON c.Customer_ID = o.Customer_ID;

<u>Ommiting repeated & unneccesary tables</u>:

Select c.customer_ID,c.customer_name,o.order_ID,0.Employee_ID   from customer_Join c INNER JOIN Order_Join o ON c.Customer_ID = o.Customer_ID;

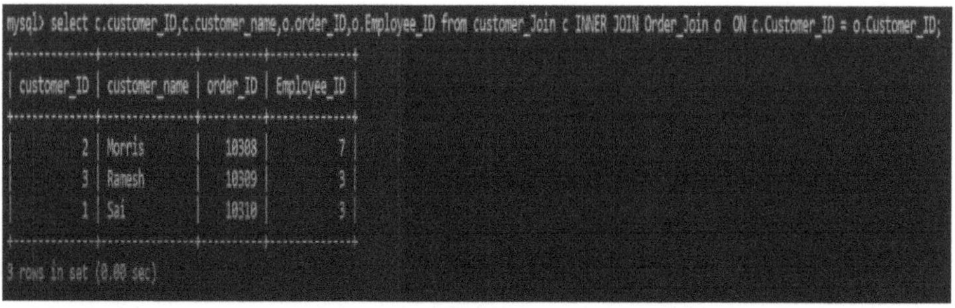

```
mysql> select c.customer_ID,c.customer_name,o.order_ID,o.Employee_ID from customer_Join c INNER JOIN Order_Join o  ON c.Customer_ID = o.Customer_ID;
+-------------+---------------+----------+-------------+
| customer_ID | customer_name | order_ID | Employee_ID |
+-------------+---------------+----------+-------------+
|           2 | Morris        |    10308 |           7 |
|           3 | Ramesh        |    10309 |           3 |
|           1 | Sai           |    10310 |           3 |
+-------------+---------------+----------+-------------+
3 rows in set (0.00 sec)
```

We can use just JOIN instead of INNER JOIN:

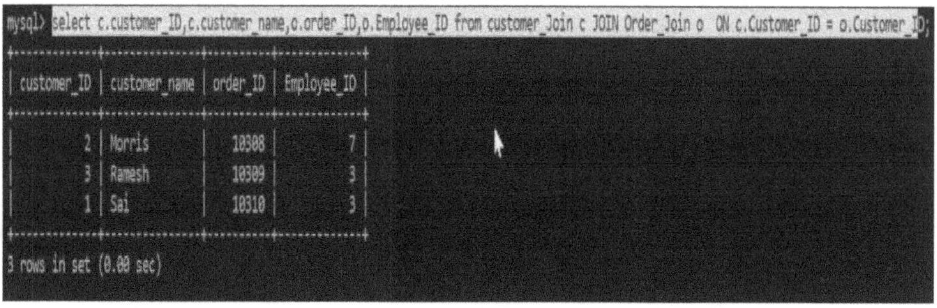

```
mysql> select c.customer_ID,c.customer_name,o.order_ID,o.Employee_ID from customer_Join c JOIN Order_Join o  ON c.Customer_ID = o.Customer_ID;
+-------------+---------------+----------+-------------+
| customer_ID | customer_name | order_ID | Employee_ID |
+-------------+---------------+----------+-------------+
|           2 | Morris        |    10308 |           7 |
|           3 | Ramesh        |    10309 |           3 |
|           1 | Sai           |    10310 |           3 |
+-------------+---------------+----------+-------------+
3 rows in set (0.00 sec)
```

We can also use "Where" condition also:

```
mysql> select c.customer_ID,c.customer_name,o.order_ID,o.Employee_ID from customer_Join c JOIN Order_Join o  ON c.Customer_ID = o.Customer_ID where o.employee_ID > 4;
+-------------+---------------+----------+-------------+
| customer_ID | customer_name | order_ID | Employee_ID |
+-------------+---------------+----------+-------------+
|           2 | Morris        |    10308 |           7 |
+-------------+---------------+----------+-------------+
1 row in set (0.00 sec)
```

LEFT JOIN:

Select * from customer_Join c LEFT JOIN ORDER_JOIN o ON c.Customer_ID = o.Customer_ID;

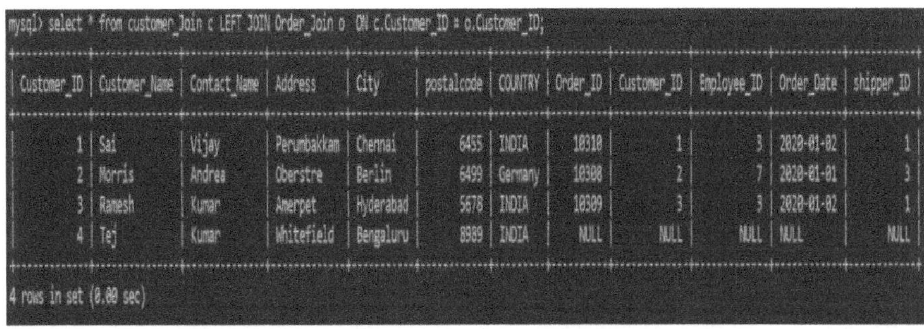

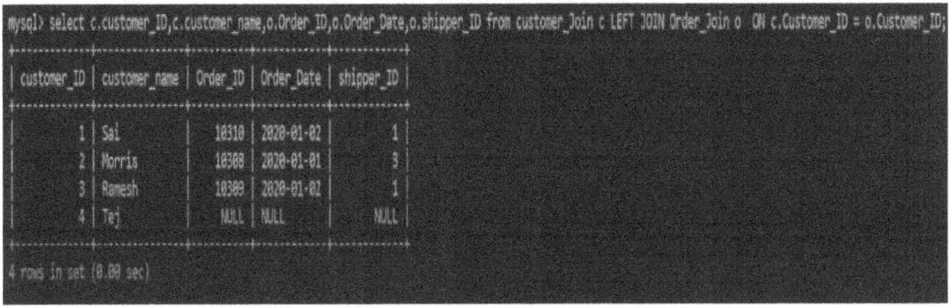

RIGHT JOIN similarly:

Select * from customer_Join c RIGHT JOIN Order_Join o ON c.Customer_ID = o.Customer_ID;

```
mysql> select * from customer_Join c RIGHT JOIN Order_Join o  ON c.Customer_ID = o.Customer_ID;
```

Customer_ID	Customer_Name	Contact_Name	Address	City	postalcode	COUNTRY	Order_ID	C
2	Morris	Andrea	Oberstre	Berlin	6499	Germany	10308	
3	Ramesh	Kumar	Amerpet	Hyderabad	5678	INDIA	10309	
1	Sai	Vijay	Perumbakkam	Chennai	6455	INDIA	10310	

```
3 rows in set (0.00 sec)
```

```
mysql> select * from order_Join o RIGHT JOIN customer_Join c  ON o.Customer_ID = c.Customer_ID;
+----------+-------------+-------------+------------+-----------+-------------+---------------+---
| Order_ID | Customer_ID | Employee_ID | Order_Date | shipper_ID | Customer_ID | Customer_Name | C
+----------+-------------+-------------+------------+-----------+-------------+---------------+---
|    10310 |           1 |           3 | 2020-01-02 |         1 |           1 | Sai           | V
|    10308 |           2 |           7 | 2020-01-01 |         3 |           2 | Morris        | A
|    10309 |           3 |           3 | 2020-01-02 |         1 |           3 | Ramesh        | K
|     NULL |        NULL |        NULL | NULL       |      NULL |           4 | Tej           | K
+----------+-------------+-------------+------------+-----------+-------------+---------------+---
4 rows in set (0.00 sec)
```

```
mysql> select * from order_Join o RIGHT JOIN customer_Join c  ON o.Customer_ID = c.Customer_ID order by c.employee_ID;
ERROR 1054 (42S22): Unknown column 'c.employee_ID' in 'order clause'
mysql> select * from order_Join o RIGHT JOIN customer_Join c  ON o.Customer_ID = c.Customer_ID order by c.Employee_ID;
ERROR 1054 (42S22): Unknown column 'c.Employee_ID' in 'order clause'
mysql> select * from order_Join o RIGHT JOIN customer_Join c  ON o.Customer_ID = c.Customer_ID order by o.Employee_ID;
+----------+-------------+-------------+------------+-----------+-------------+---------------+--------------+---------
| Order_ID | Customer_ID | Employee_ID | Order_Date | shipper_ID | Customer_ID | Customer_Name | Contact_Name | Address
+----------+-------------+-------------+------------+-----------+-------------+---------------+--------------+---------
|     NULL |        NULL |        NULL | NULL       |      NULL |           4 | Tej           | Kumar        | Whitefi
|    10310 |           1 |           3 | 2020-01-02 |         1 |           1 | Sai           | Vijay        | Perumba
|    10309 |           3 |           3 | 2020-01-02 |         1 |           3 | Ramesh        | Kumar        | Amerpet
|    10308 |           2 |           7 | 2020-01-01 |         3 |           2 | Morris        | Andrea       | Oberstr
+----------+-------------+-------------+------------+-----------+-------------+---------------+--------------+---------
4 rows in set (0.01 sec)
```

OUTER JOIN:

In MySQL, FULL OUTER JOIN cannot be possible as it won't allow.

CROSS JOIN:

```
mysql> select * from order_Join o CROSS JOIN customer_Join c  ON o.Customer_ID = c.Customer_ID order by o.Employee_ID;
+----------+-------------+-------------+------------+-----------+-------------+---------------+--------------+---------
| Order_ID | Customer_ID | Employee_ID | Order_Date | shipper_ID | Customer_ID | Customer_Name | Contact_Name | Address
+----------+-------------+-------------+------------+-----------+-------------+---------------+--------------+---------
|    10309 |           3 |           3 | 2020-01-02 |         1 |           3 | Ramesh        | Kumar        | Amerpet
|    10310 |           1 |           3 | 2020-01-02 |         1 |           1 | Sai           | Vijay        | Perumbak
|    10308 |           2 |           7 | 2020-01-01 |         3 |           2 | Morris        | Andrea       | Oberstre
+----------+-------------+-------------+------------+-----------+-------------+---------------+--------------+---------
3 rows in set (0.00 sec)
```

```
mysql> select * from order_Join o CROSS JOIN customer_Join c ;
+----------+-------------+-------------+------------+-----------+-------------+---------------+
| Order_ID | Customer_ID | Employee_ID | Order_Date | shipper_ID | Customer_ID | Customer_Name |
+----------+-------------+-------------+------------+-----------+-------------+---------------+
|    10310 |           1 |           3 | 2020-01-02 |         1 |           1 | Sai           |
|    10309 |           3 |           3 | 2020-01-02 |         1 |           1 | Sai           |
|    10308 |           2 |           7 | 2020-01-01 |         3 |           1 | Sai           |
|    10310 |           1 |           3 | 2020-01-02 |         1 |           2 | Morris        |
|    10309 |           3 |           3 | 2020-01-02 |         1 |           2 | Morris        |
|    10308 |           2 |           7 | 2020-01-01 |         3 |           2 | Morris        |
|    10310 |           1 |           3 | 2020-01-02 |         1 |           3 | Ramesh        |
|    10309 |           3 |           3 | 2020-01-02 |         1 |           3 | Ramesh        |
|    10308 |           2 |           7 | 2020-01-01 |         3 |           3 | Ramesh        |
|    10310 |           1 |           3 | 2020-01-02 |         1 |           4 | Tej           |
|    10309 |           3 |           3 | 2020-01-02 |         1 |           4 | Tej           |
|    10308 |           2 |           7 | 2020-01-01 |         3 |           4 | Tej           |
+----------+-------------+-------------+------------+-----------+-------------+---------------+
12 rows in set (0.01 sec)
```

Create View from Existing Table:

```
mysql> create view simple_join as select * from customer_Join;
Query OK, 0 rows affected (0.01 sec)

mysql> select * from simple_join;
+-------------+---------------+--------------+-------------+-----------+------------+---------+
| Customer_ID | Customer_Name | Contact_Name | Address     | City      | postalcode | COUNTRY |
+-------------+---------------+--------------+-------------+-----------+------------+---------+
|           1 | Sai           | Vijay        | Perumbakkam | Chennai   |       6455 | INDIA   |
|           2 | Morris        | Andrea       | Oberstre    | Berlin    |       6499 | Germany |
|           3 | Ramesh        | Kumar        | Amerpet     | Hyderabad |       5678 | INDIA   |
|           4 | Tej           | Kumar        | Whitefield  | Bengaluru |       8989 | INDIA   |
+-------------+---------------+--------------+-------------+-----------+------------+---------+
4 rows in set (0.00 sec)
```

SQL SUB QUERY

Sub Query is a Query within another Query. There are 2 types of Sub Queries:

1) Single Row sub query
2) Multi Row sub query

In other words, A Subquery or Inner query or a Nested query is a query within another SQL query and embedded within the WHERE clause. A subquery is used to return data that will be used in the main query as a condition to further restrict the data to be retrieved.

Subqueries can be used with the SELECT, INSERT, UPDATE, and DELETE statements along with the operators like =, <, >, >=, <=, IN, BETWEEN, etc.

- A subquery may occur in :
    - - A SELECT clause
    - - A FROM clause
    - - A WHERE clause

Subqueries are most frequently used with the SELECT statement. The basic syntax is as follows −

- SELECT column_name [, column_name]
- FROM table1 [, table2]
- WHERE column_name OPERATOR
- (SELECT column_name [, column_name]
- FROM table1 [, table2]
- [WHERE])

A subquery is also called an inner query or inner select, while the statement containing a subquery is also called an outer query or outer select. Many Transact-SQL statements that include subqueries can be alternatively formulated as joins.

Based on Outer (OQ) and Inner Queries (IQ), Sub Query is classified into 2 types:

a) <u>Non-Correlated sub query</u>:- Inner query will execute first while Outer query will execute later.

b) <u>Correlated sub query</u>: Outer query will execute first while Inner query will execute later.

See the Example below in Database ***to find the Employee who is having maximum salary***.

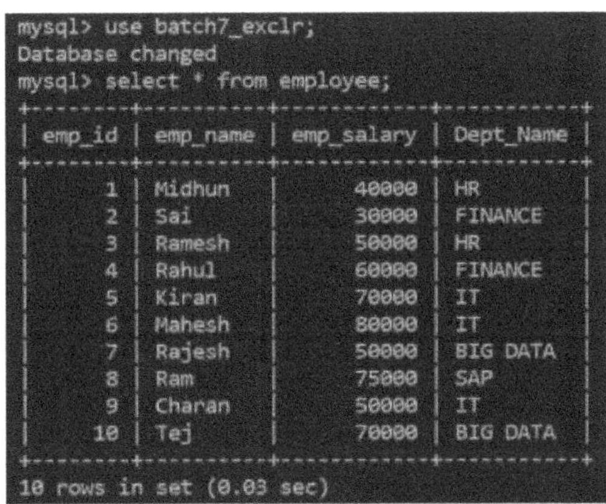

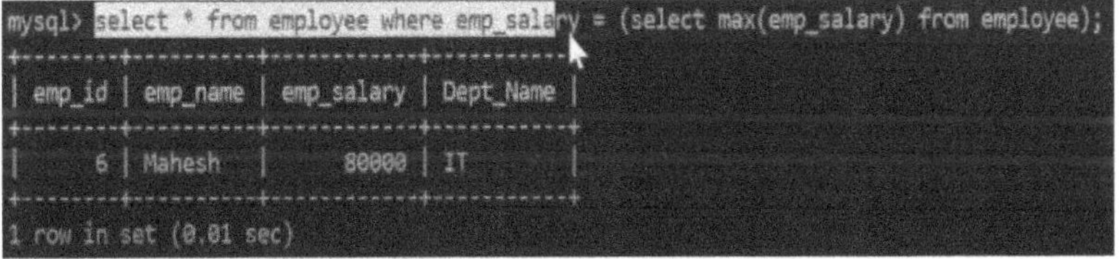

Here,

Outer Query is select * from employee where emp_salary

Inner Query is (select max(emp_salary) from employee)

First, Inner Query will be executed, and then later Output will be given to Outer Query.

SQL Stored Procedures (SPS)

A SQL stored procedure (SP) is a collection SQL statements and SQL command logic, which is compiled and stored on the database. A stored procedure in SQL allows us to create SQL queries to be stored and executed on the server. Stored procedures can also be cached and reused.

The main purpose of stored procedures is to hide direct SQL queries from the code and improve performance of database operations such as select, update, and delete data.

Stored Procedures are created to perform one or more DML operations on Database. SQL stored procedures increase productivity and manageability in application development by providing means for

a) Storing parts of application logic, encapsulated in the database, and to be used by multiple programs and multiple programmers, allowing also logic maintenance centrally in a single place. Stored routines should be written by experienced developers because they may be used in different transactions which make it difficult to develop and test.

b) Security as the used data access privileges are needed only from the professional creators (with create procedure privilege) of the procedures, and only execution privilege need to be granted per procedure to proper user groups. Also SQL injection possibilities are eliminated on part of stored procedures.

   c) Performance benefits in minimizing package preparation (parsing and binding) work, and reducing network traffic from remote clients, but also decreasing context switching, when several SQL statements can be included in a package.
   d) Productivity in data access programming by extending the SQL language with procedural flow of control and sub-

programming techniques familiar from the traditional block structured programming languages.

The SQL procedure language allows programming stored routines which contain SQL statements with elements known from traditional block structured 3GL programming languages including:

• Polymorphism with SQL parameters of IN, OUT, INOUT modes • Procedure Call statements
• Function invocations and RETURN statement
• BEGIN [ATOMIC] – END blocks
• Declared local SQL variables (of SQL data types)
• Assignment statements of the form "SET variable = expression"
• Conditional control structures IF and CASE
• Labelling of statements with ITERATE and LEAVE
• Looping structures LOOP, WHILE, UNTIL and FOR • SQL cursor processing • Error signalling and exception handling (Melton 1998).

There are two types of stored procedures available in SQL Server:
    A) User defined stored procedures
    B) System stored procedures

    A) User defined stored procedures

User defined stored procedures are created by database developers or database administrators. These SPs contains one more SQL statements to select, update, or delete records from database tables. User defined stored procedure can take input parameters and return output parameters. User defined stored procedure is mixture of DDL (Data Definition Language) and DML (Data Manipulation Language) commands.

User defined SPs are further classified into two types:

T-SQL stored procedures: T-SQL (Transact SQL) SPs receive and returns parameters. These SPs process the Insert, Update and Delete queries with or without parameters and return data of rows as output. This is one of the most common ways to write SPs in SQL Server.

CLR stored procedures: CLR (Common Language Runtime) SPs are written in a CLR based programming language such as C# or VB.NET and are executed by the .NET Framework.

B) System stored procedures

System stored procedures are created and executed by SQL Server for the server administrative activities. Developers usually don't interfere with system SPs.

<u>Benefits of stored procedures</u>:

When multiple SQL statements are encapsulated in a procedure, the network traffic i.e. "round trips" between the client and server are reduced. Only the final result of the procedure will be transmitted to the client, while intermediate data is processed on the server.

Performance gets improved also since the SQL statements are parsed and optimized when the procedure is created, and the execution plans are packaged, stored in the database and cached for repeated use. The optimized machine code runs much faster than interpreted SQL-code.

Security is improved, since procedures should be created only by competent developers (definers) who are granted privileges to create procedures and who need to have all the privileges that are required for the embedded SQL statements, and users (invokers) who have execution privilege for the procedure do not need to have all those privileges that the developer needs.

The external stored routines can be written in various programming languages, compiled and the executable code is registered in system tables by the CREATE command referring to the code library. This means that procedures can be delivered without the source code. If the routines were executed directly by the server process, the whole server might be vulnerable for programming errors.

Improved maintainability means that procedures can be invoked by multiple programs, and if the procedure logic needs to be updated, it can be done "on the fly" as an atomic operation.

Stored routines ensure data access consistency and maintainability, since when some objects to be accessed are changed or deleted the execution plan of the routine is invalidated automatically.

As a benefit of stored routines, the DB2 manual "Developing User-defined Routines" mentions "interoperability of logic implemented in different programming languages". Data access APIs is available for calling SQL stored procedures from various programming languages. The SQL interface (signature) of stored routines used for accessing the external stored routines, perhaps written in different programming languages, such as Java, even extends the interoperability.

Challenges for stored procedures include their involvement and synchronization in transactions, complicated exception handling, and need for extended documentation.

Implementing whole database transactions as stored procedures requires and promotes a strict transaction programming discipline. Developing stored procedures in IDE workbenches, such as IBM Data Studio or Oracle SQL Developer, before deployment into database provide means for code debugging and Unit Testing of transactions.

SPL Rank() Function

The RANK() function is also known as window function that assigns a rank to each row within a group of data sets. The rank of a row is determined by one plus the number of ranks that come before it.

The syntax of the RANK() function is as follows
    SELECT column_name,
    RANK() OVER (PARTITION BY... ORDER BY...) as rank
    FROM table_name;

In this syntax:
The column_name represents the column that you wish to rank in the table

The PARTITION BY clause divides the result set's rows into partitions based on one or more parameters

The ORDER BY clause sorts the rows in each partition where the function is applied.

RANK() function is used as part of the SELECT statement.

Basically, you add another column to your result set. This column includes the rank of each record based on the order specified after the ORDER BY keyword. This entails specifying (1) the **column to use for sorting the rows** and (2) whether the order should be **ascending or descending**.

The first row gets rank 1, and the following rows get higher rankings. If any rows have the same value in the column used for ordering, they are ranked the same. The RANK() function leaves gaps in such cases.

<u>SQL Interview FAQ</u>

1. What is RDBMS?

Relational Data Base Management Systems (RDBMS) are database management systems that maintain data records and indices in tables. Relationships may be created and maintained across and among the data and tables. In a relational database, relationships between data items are expressed by means of tables. Interdependencies among these tables are expressed by data values rather than by pointers. This allows a high degree of data independence. An RDBMS has the capability to recombine the data items from different files, providing powerful tools for data usage.

2. What is View?

A simple view can be thought of as a subset of a table. It can be used for retrieving data, as well as updating or deleting rows. Rows updated or deleted in the view are updated or deleted in the table the view was created with. It should also be noted that as data in the original table changes, so does data in the view, as views are the way to look at part of the original table. The results of using a view are not permanently stored in the database. The data accessed through a view is actually constructed using standard T-SQL select command and can come from one to many different base tables or even other views.

In SQL, the views are classified into four types. They are:

- Simple View: A view that is based on a single table and does not have a GROUP BY clause or other features.

- Complex View: A view that is built from several tables and includes a GROUP BY clause as well as functions.

- Inline View: A view that is built on a subquery in the FROM clause, which provides a temporary table and simplifies a complicated query.

- Materialized View: A view that saves both the definition and the details. It builds data replicas by physically preserving them.

3. What is Index?

An index is a physical structure containing pointers to the data. Indices are created in an existing table to locate rows more quickly and efficiently. It is possible to create an index on one or more columns of a table, and each index is given a name. The users cannot see the indexes; they are just used to speed up queries. Effective indexes are one of the best ways to improve performance in a database application. A table scan happens when there is no index available to help a query. In a table scan SQL Server examines every row in the table to satisfy the query results. Table scans are sometimes unavoidable, but on large tables, scans have a terrific impact on performance. Clustered indexes define the physical sorting of a database table's rows in the storage media. For this reason, each database table may have only one clustered index. Non-clustered indexes are created outside of the database table and contain a sorted list of references to the table itself.

4. What are the difference between clustered and a non-clustered index?

A clustered index is a special type of index that reorders the way records in the table are physically stored. Therefore table can have only one clustered index. The leaf nodes of a clustered index contain the data pages.

A non-clustered index is a special type of index in which the logical order of the index does not match the physical stored order of the rows on disk. The leaf node of a non-clustered index does not consist of the data pages. Instead, the leaf nodes contain index rows.

5.   What are cursors?

Cursor is a database object used by applications to manipulate data in a set on a row-by-row basis, instead of the typical SQL commands that operate on all the rows in the set at one time.

6.   What is the use of DBCC commands?

DBCC stands for database consistency checker. We use these commands to check the consistency of the databases, i.e., maintenance, validation task and status checks. E.g. DBCC CHECKDB - Ensures that tables in the db and the indexes are correctly linked.
DBCC CHECKALLOC - To check that all pages in a db are correctly allocated. DBCC CHECKFILEGROUP - Checks all tables file group for any damage.

7.   What is a Linked Server?

Linked Servers is a concept in SQL Server by which we can add other SQL Server to a Group and query both the SQL Server dbs using T-SQL Statements. With a linked server, you can create very clean, easy to follow, SQL statements that allow remote data to be retrieved, joined and combined with local data. Storped Procedure sp_addlinkedserver, sp_addlinkedsrvlogin will be used add new Linked Server.

8.   What's the difference between a primary key and a unique key?

Both Primary key and unique key enforce uniqueness of the column on which they are defined. But by default primary key creates a clustered index on the column, where are unique creates a non-clustered index by default. Another major difference is that, primary key doesn't allow NULLs, but unique key allows one NULL only.

9. What is difference between DELETE & TRUNCATE commands?

Delete command removes the rows from a table based on the condition that we provide with a WHERE clause.

Truncate will actually remove all the rows from a table and there will be no data in the table after we run the truncate command.

10. Difference between Function and Stored Procedure?

UDF can be used in the SQL statements anywhere in the WHERE/HAVING/SELECT section where as Stored procedures cannot be. UDFs that return tables can be treated as another row set. This can be used in JOINs with other tables. Inline UDF's can be thought of as views that take parameters and can be used in JOINs and other Row set operations.

11. What types of Joins are possible with Sql Server?

Joins are used in queries to explain how different tables are related. Joins also let you select data from a table depending upon data from another table. Types of joins: INNER JOINs, OUTER JOINs, CROSS JOINs. OUTER JOINs are further classified as LEFT OUTER JOINS, RIGHT OUTER JOINS and FULL OUTER JOINS.

12. What is the difference between a HAVING CLAUSE and a WHERE CLAUSE?

Specifies a search condition for a group or an aggregate. HAVING can be used only with the SELECT statement. HAVING is typically used in a GROUP BY clause. When GROUP BY is not used, HAVING behaves like a WHERE clause. Having Clause is basically used only with the GROUP BY function in a query. WHERE Clause is applied to each row before they are part of the GROUP BY function in a query.

13. What is SQL Profiler?

SQL Profiler is a graphical tool that allows system administrators to monitor events in an instance of Microsoft SQL Server. You can capture and save data about each event to a file or SQL Server table to analyze later. For example, you can monitor a production environment to see which stored procedures are hampering performances by executing too slowly.

14. What is User Defined Functions?

User-Defined Functions allow defining its own T-SQL functions that can accept 0 or more parameters and return a single scalar data value or a table data type.

There are three types of User-Defined functions in SQL Server 2000 and they are Scalar, Inline Table Valued and Multi-statement Table-valued.

A Scalar user-defined function returns one of the scalar data types. Text, ntext, image and timestamp data types are not supported. These are the type of user-defined functions that most developers are used to in other programming languages. You pass in 0 to many parameters and you get a return value.

An Inline Table-Value user-defined function returns a table data type and is an exceptional alternative to a view as the user-defined function can pass parameters into a T-SQL select command and in essence provide us with a parameterized, non-updateable view of the underlying tables.

A Multi-Statement Table-Value user-defined function returns a table and is also an exceptional alternative to a view as the function can support multiple T-SQL statements to build the final result where the view is limited to a single SELECT statement. Also, the ability to pass parameters into a T SQL select command or a group of them gives us the capability to in essence create a parameterized, non-updateable view of the data in the underlying tables. Within the create function command you must define the table structure that is being returned. After creating this type of user-defined function, It can be used in the FROM clause of a T-SQL command unlike the behavior found when using a stored procedure which can also return record sets.

15. Which TCP/IP port does SQL Server run on? How can it be changed?

SQL Server runs on port 1433. It can be changed from the Network Utility TCP/IP properties –> Port number, both on client and the server.

16. What are the authentication modes in SQL Server? How can it be changed?

Windows mode and mixed mode (SQL & Windows). To change authentication mode in SQL Server click Start, Programs, Microsoft SQL Server and click SQL Enterprise Manager to run SQL Enterprise Manager from the Microsoft SQL Server program group. Select the server then from the Tools menu select SQL Server Configuration Properties, and choose the Security page.

17. Where are SQL server users names and passwords are stored in sql server?

They get stored in master db in the sysxlogins table.

18. What is SQL server agent?

SQL Server agent plays an important role in the day-to-day tasks of a database administrator (DBA). It is often overlooked as one of the main tools for SQL Server management. Its purpose is to ease the implementation of tasks for the DBA, with its full-function scheduling engine, which allows you to schedule your own jobs and scripts.

19. What is the difference between a local and a global variable?

A local temporary table exists only for the duration of a connection or, if defined inside a compound statement, for the duration of the compound statement.

A global temporary table remains in the database permanently, but the rows exist only within a given connection. When connections are closed, the data in the global temporary table disappears. However, the table definition remains with the database for access when database is opened next time.

20. What are the different types of replication? Explain.

The SQL Server 2000-supported replication types are as follows:
• Transactional
• Snapshot
• Merge

Snapshot replication distributes data exactly as it appears at a specific moment in time and does not monitor for updates to the data. Snapshot replication is best used as a method for replicating data that change infrequently or where the most up-to-date values (low latency) are not a requirement. When synchronization occurs, the entire snapshot is generated and sent to Subscribers.

Transactional replication, an initial snapshot of data is applied at Subscribers, and then when data modifications are made at the Publisher, the individual transactions are captured and propagated to Subscribers.

Merge replication is the process of distributing data from Publisher to Subscribers, allowing the Publisher and Subscribers to make updates while connected or disconnected, and then merging the updates between sites when they are connected.

21. What are the OS services that the SQL Server installation adds?

MS SQL SERVER SERVICE, SQL AGENT SERVICE, DTC (Distribution transac co-ordinator)

22. What are three SQL keywords used to change or set someone's permissions?

GRANT, DENY, and REVOKE.

23. What are primary keys and foreign keys?

Primary keys are the unique identifiers for each row. They must contain unique values and cannot be null. Due to their importance in relational databases, Primary keys are the most fundamental of all keys and constraints. A table can have only one Primary key.

Foreign keys are both a method of ensuring data integrity and a manifestation of the relationship between tables.

24. What is the basic functions for master, msdb, model, tempdb databases?

The Master database holds information for all databases located on the SQL Server instance and is the glue that holds the engine together. Because SQL Server cannot start without a functioning master database, you must administer this database with care.

The msdb database stores information regarding database backups, SQL Agent information, DTS packages, SQL Server jobs, and some replication information such as for log shipping.

The tempdb holds temporary objects such as global and local temporary tables and stored procedures. The model is essentially a template database used in the creation of any new user database created in the instance.

25. What is data integrity? Explain constraints?

Data integrity is an important feature in SQL Server. When used properly, it ensures that data is accurate, correct, and valid. It also acts as a trap for otherwise undetectable bugs within applications.

A PRIMARY KEY constraint is a unique identifier for a row within a database table. Every table should have a primary key constraint to uniquely identify each row and only one primary key constraint can be created for each table. The primary key constraints are used to enforce entity integrity.

A UNIQUE constraint enforces the uniqueness of the values in a set of columns, so no duplicate values are entered. The unique key constraints are used to enforce entity integrity as the primary key constraints.

A FOREIGN KEY constraint prevents any actions that would destroy links between tables with the corresponding data values. A foreign key in one table points to a primary key in another table. Foreign keys prevent actions that would leave rows with foreign key values when there are no primary keys with that value. The foreign key constraints are used to enforce referential integrity.

26. What are the properties of the Relational tables?

Relational tables have six properties:
• Values are atomic.
• Column values are of the same kind.
• Each row is unique.
• The sequence of columns is insignificant.

• The sequence of rows is insignificant. • Each column must have a unique name.

27. What is De-normalization?

De-normalization is the process of attempting to optimize the performance of a database by adding redundant data. It is sometimes necessary because current DBMSs implement the relational model poorly. A true relational DBMS would allow for a fully normalized database at the logical level, while providing physical storage of data that is tuned for high performance. De-normalization is a technique to move from higher to lower normal forms of database modelling in order to speed up database access.

28. How do you load large data to the SQL server database?

BulkCopy (BCP) is a tool used to copy huge amount of data from tables. BULK INSERT command helps to Imports a data file into a database table or view in a user-specified format.

29. What is Self-Join?

This is a particular case when one table joins to itself, with one or two aliases to avoid confusion. A self-join can be of any type, as long as the joined tables are the same. A self-join is rather unique in that it involves a relationship with only one table. The common example is when company have a hierarchal reporting structure whereby one member of staff reports to another.

30. What is Cross Join?

A cross join that does not have a WHERE clause produces the Cartesian product of the tables involved in the join. The size of a Cartesian product result set is the number of rows in the first table multiplied by the number of rows in the second table. The common example is when company wants to combine each product with a pricing table to analyze each product at each price.

31. What is OLTP (OnLine Transaction Processing)?

In OLTP - online transaction processing systems relational database design use the discipline of data modelling and generally follow the Code rules of data normalization in order to ensure absolute data integrity. Using these rules complex information is broken down into its most simple structures (a table) where all of the individual atomic level elements relate to each other and satisfy the normalization rules.

32. What is an execution plan? When would you use it? How would you view the execution plan?

An execution plan is basically a road map that graphically or textually shows the data retrieval methods chosen by the SQL Server query optimizer for a stored procedure or ad-hoc query and is a very useful tool for a developer to understand the performance characteristics of a query or stored procedure since the plan is the one that SQL Server will place in its cache and use to execute the stored procedure or query. From within Query Analyzer is an option called "Show Execution Plan" (located on the Query drop-down menu). If this option is turned on it will display query execution plan in separate window when query is ran again.

33. What are the subsets of SQL?

SQL queries are divided into four main categories:

- ***Data Definition Language (DDL)***

  DDL queries are made up of SQL commands that can be used

  to define the structure of the database and modify it.

  - **CREATE** Creates databases, tables, schema, etc.

  - **DROP:** Drops tables and other database objects

- **DROP COLUMN:** Drops a column from any table structure
- **ALTER:** Alters the definition of database objects
- **TRUNCATE:** Removes tables, views, procedures, and other database objects
- **ADD COLUMN:** Adds any column to the table schema

- ***Data Manipulation Language (DML)***

These SQL queries are used to manipulate data in a database.

- **SELECT INTO:** Selects data from one table and inserts it into another
- **INSERT:** Inserts data or records into a table
- **UPDATE:** Updates the value of any record in the database
- **DELETE:** Deletes records from a table

- ***Data Control Language (DCL)***

These SQL queries manage the access rights and permission control of the database.

- **GRANT:** Grants access rights to database objects
- **REVOKE:** Withdraws permission from database objects

- ***Transaction Control Language (TCL)***

TCL is a set of commands that essentially manages the transactions in a database and the changes made by the DML statements. TCL allows statements to be grouped together into logical transactions.

- o **COMMIT:** Commits an irreversible transaction, i.e., the previous image of the database prior to the transaction cannot be retrieved

- o **ROLLBACK:** Reverts the steps in a transaction in case of an error

- o **SAVEPOINT:** Sets a savepoint in the transaction to which rollback can be executed

- o **SET TRANSACTION:** Sets the characteristics of the transaction

34. What are the applications of SQL?

The major applications of SQL include:

- Writing data integration scripts

- Setting and running analytical queries

- Retrieving subsets of information within a database for analytics applications and transaction processing

- Adding, updating, and deleting rows and columns of data in a database.

35. What are the usages of SQL?

The following operations can be performed by using SQL database:

- Creating new databases

- Inserting new data

- Deleting existing data
- Updating records
- Retrieving the data
- Creating and dropping tables
- Creating functions and views
- Converting data types

36. What are SQL operators?

<u>SQL operators</u> are the special keywords or characters that perform specific operations. They are also used in SQL queries. These operators can be used within the WHERE clause of SQL commands. Based on the specified condition, SQL operators filter the data.

The SQL operators can be categorized into the following types:

- Arithmetic Operators: For mathematical operations on numerical data
  - addition (+)
  - subtraction (-)
  - multiplication (*)
  - division (/)
  - Remainder/modulus (%)

- Logical Operators: For evaluating the expressions and return results in True or False
  - ALL
  - AND

- o   ANY
- o   ISNULL
- o   EXISTS
- o   BETWEEN
- o   IN
- o   LIKE
- o   NOT
- o   OR
- o   UNIQUE

- **Comparison Operators:** For comparisons of two values and checking whether they are the same or not
  - o   equal to (=)
  - o   not equal to (!= or <>)
  - o   less than (<),
  - o   greater than (>)
  - o   less than or equal to (<=)
  - o   greater than or equal to (>=)
  - o   not less than (!<)
  - o   not greater than (!>)

- **Bitwise Operators:** For bit manipulations between two expressions of integer type. It first performs conversion of integers into binary bits and then applied operators
  - o   AND (& symbol)
  - o   OR (|, ^)

- o   NOT (~)

- •   Compound Operators: For operations on a variable before setting the variable's result to the operation's result

  - o   Add equals (+=)

  - o   subtract equals (-=)

  - o   multiply equals (*=)

  - o   divide equals (/=)

  - o   modulo equals (%=)

- •   String Operators: For concatenation and pattern matching of strings

  - o   + (String concatenation)

  - o   += (String concatenation assignment)

  - o   % (Wildcard)

  - o   [] (Character(s) matches)

  - o   [^] (Character(s) not to match)

  - o   _ (Wildcard match one character)

37. What is the ACID property in a database?

The full form of ACID is atomicity, consistency, isolation, and durability. ACID properties are used to check the reliability of transactions.

- •

- o Atomicity refers to completed or failed transactions, where a transaction refers to a single logical operation on data. This implies that if any aspect of a transaction fails, the whole transaction fails and the database state remains unchanged.

- Consistency means that the data meets all validity guidelines. The transaction never leaves the database without finishing its state.

- Concurrency management is the primary objective of isolation.

- Durability ensures that once a transaction is committed, it will occur regardless of what happens in between such as a power outage, fire, or some other kind of disturbance.

38. What is the need for group functions in SQL?

Group functions operate on a series of rows and return a single result for each group. COUNT(), MAX(), MIN(), SUM(), AVG(), and VARIANCE() are some of the most widely used group functions.

39. What is AUTO_INCREMENT?

AUTO_INCREMENT is used in SQL to automatically generate a unique number whenever a new record is inserted into a table.

Since the primary key is unique for each record, this primary field is added as the AUTO_INCREMENT field so that it is incremented when a new record is inserted.

The AUTO-INCREMENT value starts from 1 and is incremented by 1 whenever a new record is inserted.

40. What is the COALESCE function?

The COALESCE function takes a set of inputs and returns the first non-null value.

<u>Learn Data Analysis</u>:

https://skdatashare.blogspot.com/